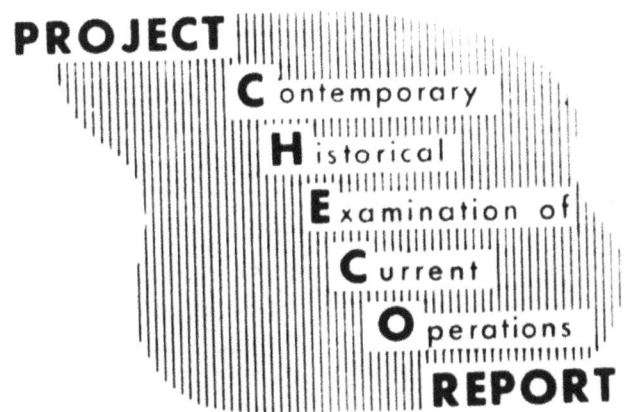

COMMANDO HUNT VI

7 JULY 1972

HQ PACAF

Directorate of Operations Analysis
CHECO/CORONA HARVEST DIVISION

DEPARTMENT OF THE AIR FORCE
HEADQUARTERS PACIFIC AIR FORCES
APO SAN FRANCISCO 96553

OFFICE OF THE CHIEF OF STAFF

PROJECT CHECO REPORTS

The counterinsurgency and unconventional warfare environment of Southeast Asia has resulted in the employment of USAF airpower to meet a multitude of requirements. The varied applications of airpower have involved the full spectrum of USAF aerospace vehicles, support equipment, and manpower. As a result, there has been an accumulation of operational data and experiences that, as a priority, must be collected, documented, and analyzed as to current and future impact upon USAF policies, concepts, and doctrine.

Fortunately, the value of collecting and documenting our SEA experiences was recognized at an early date. In 1962, Hq USAF directed CINCPACAF to establish an activity that would be primarily responsive to Air Staff requirements and direction, and would provide timely and analytical studies of USAF combat operations in SEA.

Project CHECO, an acronym for Contemporary Historical Examination of Current Operations, was established to meet this Air Staff requirement. Managed by Hq PACAF, with elements at Hq 7AF and 7/13AF, Project CHECO provides a scholarly, "on-going" historical examination, documentation, and reporting on USAF policies, concepts, and doctrine in PACOM. This CHECO report is part of the overall documentation and examination which is being accomplished. It is an authentic source for an assessment of the effectiveness of USAF airpower in PACOM when used in proper context. The reader must view the study in relation to the events and circumstances at the time of its preparation--recognizing that it was prepared on a contemporary basis which restricted perspective and that the author's research was limited to records available within his local headquarters area.

JOHN M. McNABB, Major General, USAF
Chief of Staff

DEPARTMENT OF THE AIR FORCE
HEADQUARTERS PACIFIC AIR FORCES
APO SAN FRANCISCO 96553

REPLY TO
ATTN OF: DOAD　　　　　　　　　　　　　　　　　　　　7 July 1972

SUBJECT: Project CHECO Report, "COMMANDO HUNT VI"

TO: SEE DISTRIBUTION PAGE

1. Attached is a SECRET NOFORN document. It shall be transported, stored, safeguarded, and accounted for in accordance with applicable security directives. SPECIAL HANDLING REQUIRED, NOT RELEASABLE TO FOREIGN NATIONALS. The information contained in this document will not be disclosed to foreign nations or their representatives. Retain or destroy in accordance with AFR 205-1. Do not return.

2. This letter does not contain classified information and may be declassified if attachment is removed from it.

FOR THE COMMANDER IN CHIEF

Robert E. Hiller

ROBERT E. HILLER　　　　　　　　　　　1 Atch
Director of Operations Analysis　　　Proj CHECO Rprt (S/NF),
DCS/Operations　　　　　　　　　　　　 7 Jul 72

DISTRIBUTION LIST

1. SECRETARY OF THE AIR FORCE

    a. SAFAA 1
    b. SAFLL 1
    c. SAFOI 2
    d. SAFUS 1

2. HEADQUARTERS USAF

    a. AFNB 1

    b. AFCCS
        (1) AFCCN 1
        (2) AFCVC 1
        (3) AFCHOS 2

    c. AFCSA
        (1) AFSAG 1
        (2) AFSAMI 1

    d. AFSAMA 2

    e. AFIGO
        (1) AFOSI/IVOA 3
        (2) IGS 1

    f. AFINATC 5

    g. AFACMI 1

    h. AFODC
        (1) AFPRC 1
        (2) AFPRE 1
        (3) AFPRM 1

    i. AFPDC
        (1) AFDPW 1

    j. AFRD
        (1) AFRDP 1
        (2) AFRDQ 1
        (3) AFQPC 1
        (4) AFRDR 1
        (5) AFRDQL 1

    k. AFSDC
        (1) AFLGX 1
        (2) AFLGM 1
        (3) AFLGF 1
        (4) AFLGS 1
        (5) AFSTP 1

    l. AFDAD 1

    m. AFXO 1
        (1) AFXOD 1
        (2) AFXODC 1
        (3) AFXODD 1
        (4) AFXODL 1
        (5) AFXOOG 1
        (6) AFXOOSL 1
        (7) AFXOV 1
        (8) AFXOOSN 1
        (9) AFXOOSO 1
        (10) AFXOOSS 1
        (11) AFXOOSV 1
        (12) AFXOOTR 1
        (13) AFXOOTW 1
        (14) AFXOOSZ 1
        (15) AFXOXAA 6
        (16) AFXOXXG 1

3. MAJOR COMMAND

   a. TAC

      (1) HEADQUARTERS
          (a) XP 1
          (b) DOC. 1
          (c) DREA 1
          (d) IN 1

      (2) AIR FORCES
          (a) 12AF
              1. DOO 1
              2. IN. 1
          (b) 19AF/IN. 1
          (c) USAFSOF/DO . . . 1

      (3) WINGS
          (a) 1SOW/DOI 1
          (b) 23TFW/DOI. . . . 1
          (c) 27TRW/DOI. . . . 1
          (d) 33TFW/DOI. . . . 1
          (e) 35TFW/DOI. . . . 1
          (f) 314TAW/DOI . . . 1
          (g) 347TRW/DOI . . . 1
          (h) 67TRW/DOI. . . . 1
          (i) 316TAW/DOX . . . 1
          (j) 363TRW/DOI . . . 1
          (k) 317TFW/DOI . . . 1
          (l) 474TFW/DOI . . . 1
          (m) 516TAW/DOX . . . 1
          (n) 4403TFW/DOI. . . 1
          (o) 58TAC FTR TNG WG 1
          (p) 354TFW/DOI . . . 1

      (4) TAC CENTERS, SCHOOLS
          (a) USAFTAWC/IN. . . 1
          (b) USAFTFWC/DR. . . 1
          (c) USAFAGOS/EDA . . 1

   b. SAC

      (1) HEADQUARTERS
          (a) DOX 1
          (b) XPX 1
          (c) LG. 1
          (d) IN. 1
          (e) NR. 1
          (f) HO. 1

      (2) AIR FORCES
          (a) 2AF/INA 1
          (b) 8AF/DOA 2
          (c) 15/INCE 1

   c. MAC

      (1) HEADQUARTERS
          (a) DOI 1
          (b) DOO 1
          (c) CSEH. 1
          (d) MACOA 1
          (e) 60MAWG/DOXPI. . . . 1

      (2) MAC SERVICES
          (a) AWS/HO. 1
          (b) ARRS/XP 1

   d. ADC

      (1) HEADQUARTERS
          (a) DO. 1
          (b) DOT 1
          (c) XPC 1

      (2) AIR DIVISIONS
          (a) 25AD/DOI. 1
          (b) 23AD/DOI. 1
          (c) 20AD/DOI. 1

   e. ATC
      (1) DOSPI 1
      (2) DPX 1

f. AFLC

   (1) HEADQUARTERS
      (a) XOX 1

g. AFSC

   (1) HEADQUARTERS
      (a) XRP 1
      (b) XRLW. 1
      (c) SAMSO/XRS 1
      (d) SDA 1
      (e) HO. 1
      (f) ASD/RWST. 1
      (g) ESD/XRL 1
      (h) RADC/DOT. 1
      (i) ADTC/CCN. 1
      (j) ADTC/DLOSL. 1
      (k) ESD/YWA 1
      (l) AFATL/DL. 1

h. USAFSS

   (1) HEADQUARTERS
      (a) AFSCC/SUR 2

   (2) SUBORDINATE UNITS
      (a) Eur Scty Rgn/DOAA . . 1

i. USAFSO

   (1) HEADQUARTERS
      (a) CSH 1

j. PACAF

   (1) HEADQUARTERS
      (a) DP 1
      (b) IN 1
      (c) XP 2
      (d) CSH. 1
      (e) DOAD 6
      (f) DC 1
      (g) LG 1

   (2) AIR FORCES
      (a) 5AF
         1. CSH. 1
         2. XP 1
         3. DO 1
      (b) Det 8, ASD/DOASD . . 1
      (c) 7AF
         1. DO 1
         2. IN 1
         3. XP 1
         4. DOCP 1
         5. DOAC 2
      (d) 13AF
         1. CSH. 1
      (e) 7/13AF/CHECO 1

   (3) AIR DIVISIONS
      (a) 313AD/DOI. 1
      (b) 314AD/XP 2
   (2) 327AD
         1. IN 1

(4) WINGS
    (a) 8TFW/DOEA. 1
    (b) 56SOW/WHD. 1
    (c) 366TFW/DO. 1
    (d) 388TFW/DO. 1
    (e) 405TFW/DOI 1
    (f) 432TRW/DOI 1
    (g) 1st Test Sq/DA 1

(5) OTHER UNITS
    (a) Task Force ALPHA/IN . . 1
    (b) Air Force Advisory Gp/DA 1

k. USAFE

(1) HEADQUARTERS
    (a) DOA. 1
    (b) DOLO 1
    (c) DOO. 1
    (d) XP 1

(2) AIR FORCES
    (a) 3AF/DO 2
    (b) 16AF/DO. 1

(3) WINGS
    (a) 50TFW/DOA. 1
    (b) 20TFW/DOI. 1
    (c) 401TFW/DOI 1
    (d) 513TAW/DOI 1

4. SEPARATE OPERATING AGENCIES
  a. ACIC/DOP. 2
  b. AFRES/XP. 2
  c. 3825AU
    1. ACSC/DAA 1
    2. AUL(SE)-69-108 2
    3. ASI/HOA. 2
  d. ANALYTIC SERVICES, INC. . 1
  e. USAFA
    1. DFH. 1
  f. AFAG/THAILAND 1

5. MILITARY DEPARTMENT, UNIFIED AND SPECIFIED COMMANDS, AND JOINT STAFFS

    a. COMUSJAPAN/J3 1
    b. CINCPAC/J301 2
    c. CINCPACFLT/Code 321 1
    d. COMUSKOREA/ATTN: J-3 1
    e. COMUSMACTHAI/MACTJ3 1
    f. COMUSMACV/TSCO 1
    g. COMUSTDC/J3 1
    h. USCINCEUR/ECJB 1
    i. CINCLANT/CL 1
    j. CHIEF, NAVAL OPERATIONS 1
    k. COMMANDANT, MARINE CORPS/ABQ 1
    l. CINCONAD/NHSV-M 1
    m. DEPARTMENT OF THE ARMY/ASM-D 1
    n. JOINT CHIEFS OF STAFF/J3RR&A 1
    o. JSTPS 1
    p. SECRETARY OF DEFENSE/OASD/SA 1
    q. CINCSTRIKE/STS 1
    r. CINCAL/RCJ3-A 1
    s. MAAG-CHINA/AF Section/MGAF-O 1
    t. U. S. DOCUMENT OFFICE, HQ ALLIED FORCES NORTHERN EUROPE 1
    u. USMACV/MACJ031 1

6. SCHOOLS

    a. Senior USAF Representative, National War College 1
    b. Senior USAF Representative, Armed Forces Staff College 1
    c. Senior USAF Rep, Industrial College of the Armed Forces 1
    d. Senior USAF Representative, Naval Amphibious School 1
    e. Senior USAF Rep, U.S. Marine Corps Education Center 1
    f. Senior USAF Representative, U.S. Naval War College 1
    g. Senior USAF Representative, U.S. Army War College 1
    h. Senior USAF Rep, U.S. Army C&G Staff College 1
    i. Senior USAF Representative, U.S. Army Infantry School 1
    j. Senior USAF Rep, USA JFK Center for Military Assistance 1
    k. Senior USAF Representative, U.S. Army Field Artillery School . . 1
    l. Senior USAF Representative, U.S. Liaison Office 1
    m. Senior USAF Rep, U.S. Army Armor School, Comd and Staff Dept . . 1

7. SPECIAL

    a. The RAND Corporation 1
    b. U.S. Air Attache, Vientiane 1

A NOTE ABOUT THE AUTHOR

Captain Bruce P. Layton has been a Systems Analyst in the Directorate of Tactical Analysis, Deputy Chief of Staff for Operations, Headquarters Seventh Air Force since May 1971. Previous assignments included Systems Analyst, Headquarters Air Force Institute of Technology, and (Titan II) Missile Combat Crew Commander.

He received his Bachelor of Science in Mathematics from MIT in 1961, and a Master of Science, Industrial Engineering (specializing in Operations Research) from Purdue in 1970. <u>Commando Hunt VI</u> is his first publication.

TABLE OF CONTENTS

	Page
A NOTE ABOUT THE AUTHOR	ix
CHAPTER I - INTRODUCTION	1
Strategic Assessment	2
Commando Hunt VI Plan	4
Overview	5
CHAPTER II - CAMPAIGN NARRATIVE	6
Steel Tiger--Interdiction	6
Ground Activity	9
Barrel Roll	10
Republic of Vietnam	13
General Activity	13
Route 103	13
Operations	14
Level of Effort, and Evaluation of Results	17
Cambodia	21
CHAPTER III - CAMPAIGN RESULTS IN STEEL TIGER	23
The Effort Against Trucks	23
Resources	23
AC-130	23
AC-119K	24
B-57G	25
Truck Movements	25
Force Effectiveness	26
Bomb Damage Assessment (BDA) Criteria	29
Significance of Results	30
Aircraft Effectiveness	32
Effort Against Other Targets	34
Truck Parks and Storage Areas	35
Effort Against Enemy Defenses	37
Effort Against AAA	37
Attacks Against Surface-to-Air Missiles	38
Protective Reaction Strikes	38
Effort Against Lines of Communication	39
Overall Assessment	40

	Page
FOOTNOTES	41
Chapter I	41
Chapter II	41
Chapter III	43

FIGURES

I-1	Southeast Asia (Map)	3
II-1	Steel Tiger VR Sectors (Map)	8
II-2	Central Laos (Map)	11
II-3	Southern Laos - Bolovens Plateau (Map)	12
II-4	Barrel Roll (Map)	15
II-5	Republic of Vietnam (Map)	16
II-6	Northwest MR-1 (Map)	19
II-7	Route 103 Area (Map)*	20
II-8	Cambodia (Map)	22
III-1	Total Sorties and Sorties Striking Trucks (O-5)	27
III-2a	Trucks Struck per Truck Observed (O-5)	28
III-2b	Trucks Destroyed or Damaged per Truck Struck (O-5)	28
III-2c	Trucks Destroyed or Damaged per Truck Observed (O-5)	28

TABLES**

III-1	Force Performance Against Trucks (WAIS, O-5)	31
III-2	Aircraft Performance Against Trucks (WAIS, O-5)	33

APPENDICES

A.	Air Resources	46
	Strike Aircraft	46
	Sorties	46
	Hits and Losses from Enemy Defenses	47
	Other Aircraft	47
B.	Enemy Resources	66
	Personnel	66
	Lines of Communication	66

*Line numbers and locations of seeding segments are given in the (S) 7AF SEA Daily Supplemental Frag - Special Instructions.

**For explanation of source abbreviations, see bottom of page xv.

		Page
	Input Corridors	66
	Central Route Structure	67
	Exit Corridors	67
	Road Proliferation	
	Input and Throughput	67
	Input	69
	Throughput	69
	Enemy Defenses	70
	AAA	70
	SAMs	70
	MIGs	70
C.	Campaign Results in Other Areas	76
	Republic of Vietnam	76
	Ground Operations	76
	Air Operations	79
	Cambodia	80
	Ground Operations	81
	Air Operations	86
	Barrel Roll	88
	Ground Operations	89
	Air Operations	92
D.	Munitions	104
	CBU-52A/B	104
	LUU-2/B	105
	CBU-55	105
E.	Weather	106
	Transition to the Southwest Monsoon	106
	Southwest Monsoon Weather Patterns	107
	Weather During Commando Hunt VI	107
F.	Figures and Tables	115

APPENDIX FOOTNOTES

Appendix B	135
Appendix C	135
Appendix D	137
Appendix E	137

Page

APPENDIX FIGURES AND TABLES

FIGURES

A-1	Allied Bases in SEA (Map)	48
B-1	Steel Tiger Route Structure (Map)	68
B-2	North Vietnam Airfields (Map)	73
C-1	Republic of Vietnam (Map)	78
C-2	Cambodia (Map)	83
C-3	Tonle Toch Area Operations (Map)	84
C-4	CHENLA II Area of Operations (Map)	87
C-5	Barrel Roll (Map)	90
C-6	Plain of Jars Area (Map)	91
F-1	Average Effective Sensor Strings (O-5)	116
F-2	Trucks Observed and Sensor-Detected Movements (O-5)	118
F-3	Percent Sensor-Detected Movements Southbound (O-5)	119
F-4	Trucks Observed, Struck, Destroyed or Damaged (O-5)	120
F-5	Weight of Effort Against Truck Parks and Storage Areas	121
F-6	Weight of Effort Against Lines of Communications (O-5)	127

TABLES

A-1	USAF Strike Resources in Thailand, as of End of Month (CSB)	49
A-2	USAF Strike Resources in the Republic of Vietnam, as of End of Month (CSB)	50
A-3	Total Sorties Flown and Portion Flown in Steel Tiger by U.S. Strike Resources in Southeast Asia (SEADAB 13)	51
A-4	Observed Target Damage in Steel Tiger (WAIS, O-5)	53
A-5	U.S. Steel Tiger Sorties Expending Ordnance by Target Type Struck on First Strike (O-5)	54
A-6	Steel Tiger Sorties Expending Ordnance by Target Type Struck on First Strike - F-4 (O-5)	55
A-7	Steel Tiger Sorties Expending Ordnance by Target Type Struck on First Strike - F-100 (O-5)	55
A-8	Steel Tiger Sorties Expending Ordnance by Target Type Struck on First Strike - AC-119K (O-5)	56
A-9	Steel Tiger Sorties Expending Ordnance by Target Type Struck on First Strike - AC-130 (O-5)	56
A-10	Steel Tiger Sorties Expending Ordnance by Target Type Struck on First Strike - B-57 (O-5)	57

		Page
A-11	Steel Tiger Sorties Expending Ordnance by Target Type Struck on First Strike - A-1 (O-5)	57
A-12	Steel Tiger Sorties Expending Ordnance by Target Type Struck on First Strike - A-6 (O-5)	58
A-13	Steel Tiger Sorties Expending Ordnance by Target Type Struck on First Strike - A-7 (O-5)	58
A-14	Barrel Roll Sorties Expending Ordnance by Target Type Struck on First Strike - F-4 (O-5)	59
A-15	Barrel Roll Sorties Expending Ordnance by Target Type Struck on First Strike - AC-119K (O-5)	59
A-16	Barrel Roll Sorties Expending Ordnance by Target Type Struck on First Strike - AC-130 (O-5)	60
A-17	Barrel Roll Sorties Expending Ordnance by Target Type Struck on First Strike - A-1 (O-5)	60
A-18	Unit Aircraft Sortie Rates (Sorties per Possessed Aircraft) (CSB)	61
A-19	Fixed-Wing USAF Aircraft Hit and Loss Experience (WAIS, DOY Hit and Loss File)	62
A-20	USAF FAC Resources by Base, as of End of Month (CSB)	63
A-21	USAF Reconnaissance Resources by Base, as of End of Month (CSB)	64
A-22	FAC Sorties by Country, Aircraft Type (O-5), SEADAB 13)	65
B-1	Enemy Order of Battle in Laos (WAIS)	72
B-2	Input in Tons by Route (WAIS)	72
B-3	Throughput in Tons by Route (WAIS)	74
B-4	AAA Order of Battle, Average by Month (WAIS)	75
C-1	Number of Enemy-Initiated Actions in RVN (WAIS)	94
C-2	U.S. and VNAF Attack Sorties in RVN (WAIS)	95
C-3	U.S. and VNAF Attack Sorties in SEA (WAIS)	96
C-4	Allied BDA Summary in RVN (WAIS)	97
C-5	Arc Light Results in RVN (WAIS)	98
C-6	USAF and VNAF Attack Sorties in Cambodia (WAIS)	99
C-7	Results of Allied Tac Air Strikes in Cambodia (WAIS)	100
C-8	Arc Light Results in Cambodia (WAIS)	100
C-9	USAF Attack Sorties in Barrel Roll (WAIS)	101
C-10	U.S. Attack Sorties in Barrel Roll by Target Type (O-5)	102
C-11	Total U.S. BDA in Barrel Roll (WAIS)	103
E-1	Frequency, in Days, of Prevailing Cloud Conditions (WESEAO)	111
E-2	Weather Cancellations (WESEAO, SEADAB 86)	113
F-1	Trucks Observed by Month (O-5)	117
F-2	Truck Park and Storage Area Results - Tactical Air (O-5)	122

		Page
F-3	Truck Park and Storage Area Results -- Arc Light (WAIS, O-5)	123
F-4	Combat Hit and Loss Experience (WAIS, DOY Hit and Loss File)	124
F-5	Sorties and Results Against AAA (O-5)	125
F-6	Sorties and Results Against Lines of Communication -- Tactical Air (WAIS)	126
F-7	Sorties and Results Against Lines of Communication -- Arc Light (WAIS)	128
F-9	Route 103 Seeding Segments, Sensor String Numbers (Provided by 7AF [DOCP])	130
F-10	Monthly Effort Against Route 103 (SEADAB)	131
F-11	Sorties (Munitions) by Seeding Segment (SEADAB)	132
F-12	Enemy Activity in Route 103 Area (Blue Chip/Igloo White Log, 7AF [DOCP])	133
F-13	Road Construction, Route 103 (Provided by 7AF [12 RITS] LOC Team)	134

GLOSSARY 139

EXPLANATION OF ABBREVIATIONS FOR DATA SOURCES USED IN LISTS OF TABLES AND FIGURES

O-5:   Igloo White OPREP-5, published weekly by 7AF (DOYR).

WAIS: Weekly Air Intelligence Summary, Published by 7AF (INO).

CSB: Command Status Book, published monthly by 7AF (ACM).

SEADAB: Southeast Asia Data Base, maintained by 7AF (DOYR). Number after "SEADAB" specifies a standard retrieval.

WESEAO: Weather Evaluation, Southeast Asia Operations, published monthly by 1st Weather Wing.

CHAPTER I

INTRODUCTION

Interdiction of the overland flow of supplies from North Vietnam to Viet Cong and North Vietnamese forces in South Vietnam and Cambodia was a primary mission for American airpower in Southeast Asia (SEA). The primary target for air interdiction was the supply system in North Vietnam (NVN), until the bombing halt there shifted the emphasis to the logistic channel in southern Laos, the Steel Tiger area of operations. The interdiction campaigns there bore the name Commando Hunt with numerical designations that changed with the semiannual monsoon shift. Commando Hunt VI, the third southwest-monsoon, or wet-season, campaign, covered the period 15 May through 31 October 1971.

The past pattern had been for the enemy to move supplies through Steel Tiger into the Republic of Vietnam (RVN) when the weather in Laos was relatively dry. Some of these supplies had been moved through Cambodia en route to RVN; since the deposition of Prince Sihanouk in 1970, the enemy needed to use supplies against the Cambodian government as well as against RVN. With the onset of the wet season, as the road system in Laos became a quagmire, the enemy shifted his emphasis to stockpiling materiel in the NVN border areas to prepare for a logistics surge through Laos during the next dry season. The sanctuary given the enemy by the NVN bombing halt enabled him to get a running start for the dry season.

Commando Hunt VI came on the heels of the most successful dry season campaign to date, whether judged in terms of greatest observed bomb damage, lowest throughput-to-input ratio, or lowest total throughput. Thus enemy activity could be expected to be at a higher level than during previous wet seasons, in order to supply his forces in the RVN and Cambodia.

Strategic Assessment

Seventh Air Force's assessment of the strategic situation to be faced during the 1971 southwest-monsoon season was that it would be a period of continuing surveillance and air strike operations, limited by the prevailing weather conditions. Air interdiction missions would continue in those areas where heavy rainfall did not reduce the capability of the enemy's logistic system. That system was to be kept under observation, and attacked when appropriate, in Steel Tiger, Cambodia, and the Republic of Vietnam. Support was to be provided to Allied forces in the RVN, northern Laos (Barrel Roll), and Steel Tiger.[1]

The enemy's construction, road repair, and defensive activity were expected to decrease during the first months of the campaign. The antiaircraft artillery (AAA) threat was also expected to decrease in proportion to reduced resupply and interdiction activity. As the southwest-monsoon season drew to a close, the enemy was expected to increase both his AAA defenses and his resupply activities.[2]

The level of enemy activity was anticipated to be down considerably in the RVN and Cambodia from the previous wet season. However, the

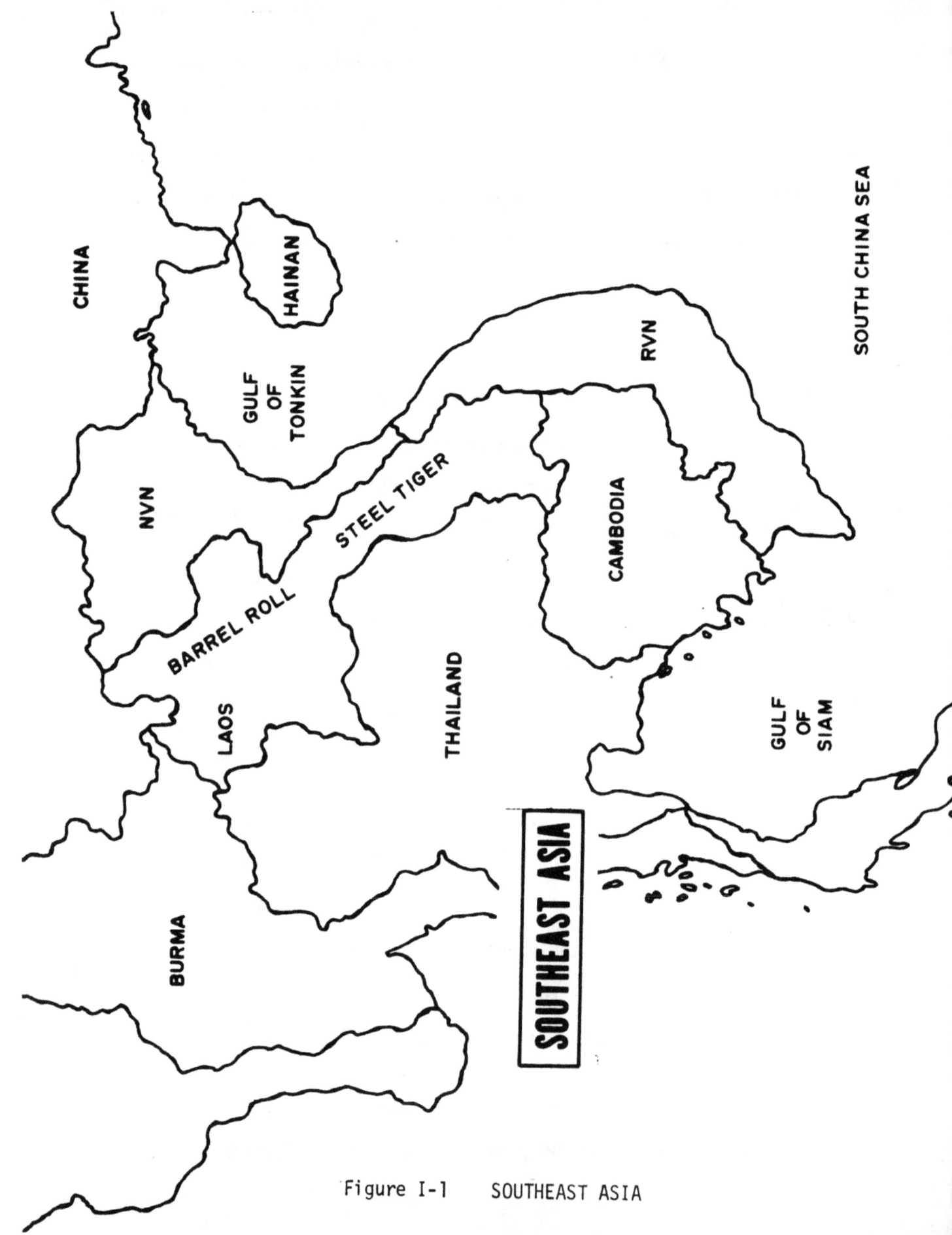

Figure I-1   SOUTHEAST ASIA

enemy logistic system in Laos was expected to be much more active than in previous campaigns. Accordingly, the probable percentage distribution of tactical aircraft (tac air) by area was determined to be: Steel Tiger - 70 per cent; Barrel Roll - 10 per cent; Cambodia - 10 per cent; and the RVN - 10 percent.[3]

Commando Hunt VI Plan

Based upon his assessment of the strategic situation, the Commander, Seventh Air Force, promulgated Seventh Air Force Operations Plan 730, the campaign plan for Commando Hunt VI. For the first time in the Commando Hunt series of campaigns, the Plan covered air operations in the RVN and Cambodia as well as in Laos.[4] The authorized level of US fighter-attack sorties when the wet season began was 14,000 per month, but the Joint Chiefs of Staff reduced the allocation for the remainder of the wet season to 10,000 per month effective 1 July 1971.[5]

As long as enemy activity warranted, the basic ingredients of the dry season interdiction campaign were to be applied. As the dry season came to a close, strikes were to be increased against interdiction points (IDPs) to hasten deterioration of the roads. Emphasis was to be placed on the forward air controller (FAC)-Quick Reaction Force (QRF) team to provide rapid response against temporary targets during periods of good weather. The plan recognized the primacy to be given to support of ground forces engaged with the enemy.[6] The Commander, US Military Assistance Command, Vietnam (COMUSMACV) approved the plan, and the plan was endorsed by the Commander-in-Chief, Pacific Air Forces (CINCPACAF).[7]

The enemy resupply activity that was characteristic of the dry season continued into May, but the level of activity was affected by the weather. Input activity continued at a reduced level while the throughput rate increased, reflecting the enemy's effort to beat the onset of the wet season. Toward the middle of May, afternoon and evening thunderstorm activity became more extensive and persistent, often lasting through the night. Based on this change in weather conditions, 15 May 1971 was designated as the beginning of Commando Hunt VI. [8/]

Overview

Chapter II contains a narrative of the Commando Hunt VI campaign. Chapter III treats the campaign in Steel Tiger in terms of its major features: the effort against trucks, and attacks against truck parks and storage areas, lines of communication (LOCs), and enemy defenses.

Detailed data on allied and enemy resources and operations are left to the appendices. Appendices also include descriptions of new weapons systems and weather factors during the campaign, along with ground and air operations in other areas.

CHAPTER II

CAMPAIGN NARRATIVE

Steel Tiger--Interdiction

During the first 14 days of May, the enemy achieved a considerable surge in throughput of supplies into the RVN and Cambodia. He was able to input an estimated 1,000 tons of supplies with a throughput-to-input ratio of about 1 to 3.5, compared to the 1 to 9 ratio for the dry season just ended. Simultaneously with the input surge, the enemy moved many of his empty trucks back into North Vietnam. Thus, when the Commando Hunt VI campaign officially opened on 15 May 1971, the truck population in Steel Tiger was considerably reduced. [9]

United States Air Force tactical air efforts in late May went primarily against the exit routes, especially the Route 922 complex in support of Lam Son 720 in the RVN. Secondary efforts were directed against Mu Gia and Ban Karai passes and the western portion of the Route 110 complex, the latter in an attempt to disrupt traffic supporting the enemy's Bolovens Plateau offensive. [10]

The deterioration of road conditions throughout Steel Tiger was indicated by the steady decrease in sensor-detected movements until the last week in June, when a turn of good weather resulted in an increase from 646 to over 900 for each of the next two weeks. Then Typhoons Harriet (7 July) and Kim (13 July) flooded the route structure so thoroughly as to reduce mover levels to below 200 per week for the rest of the campaign. The two typhoons and Tropical Storm Jean the following week made the LOCs generally impassable, so tac air emphasis shifted to striking truck parks and storage areas.[11]

On 1 July 7AF implemented a realignment of FAC Visual Reconnaissance (VR) sectors to provide improved operating areas for gunships and tac air. The realignment was intended to improve navigation, air traffic control, and visual reconnaissance.[12] (See Figure II-1, for map showing new VR sectors.)

The enemy sustained a considerable road-improvement program in Steel Tiger throughout the wet season, presumably to permit an earlier movement of supplies southward once the dry season began. In late September the amount of traffic began to increase, as did the amount of road construction. However, enemy efforts were set back when Tropical Storms Della (1 Oct) and Elaine (9 Oct) rendered all entries to Steel Tiger impassable until 13 October. Then enemy activity stepped up again until Typhoon Hester reached there on 23 October. There was no activity that day, but within a week the traffic had risen to the level present before Hester. In spite of the much lower level of activity described above, weather cover had reduced tac air effectiveness so that the throughput-to-input ratio remained at about 1 to 3.5 for the entire wet season.[13]

When it was evident that the northeast monsoon was fairly established, and with no further slowdown of the enemy's logistic campaign in sight, 1 November was designated as the beginning of Commando Hunt VII for statistical purposes. At this time, Ban Karai Pass was still closed and traffic had just begun to flow again in Mu Gia Pass.[14]

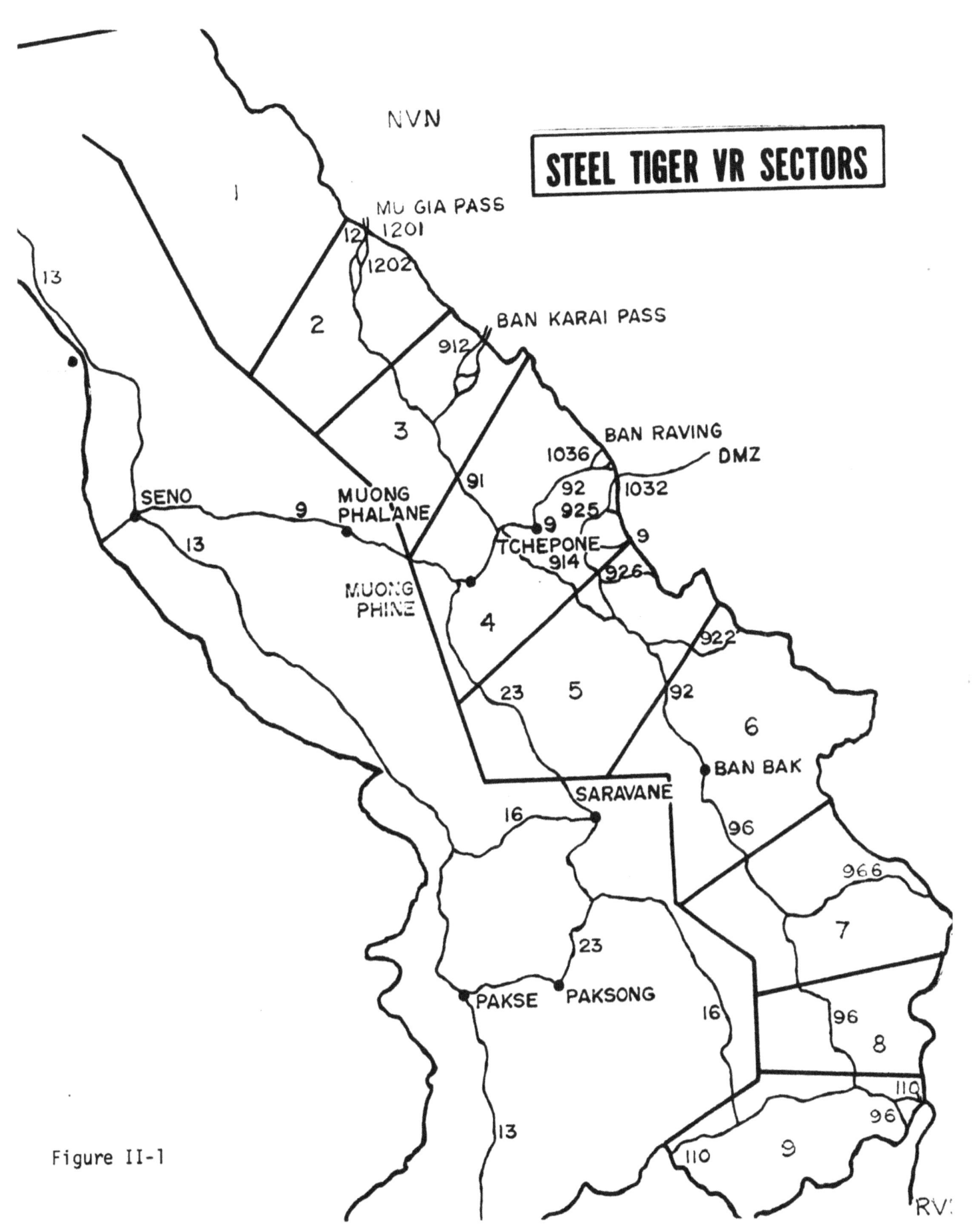
Figure II-1

Ground Activity

In central Laos, the enemy threatened, in May, to take Seno and cut off the Royal Laotian Government (RLG) line of communication between northern and southern Laos. However, in early June the RLG began an advance that reached Muong Phalane in about a month. For the rest of the Commando Hunt VI campaign the RLG force remained near Muong Phalane, but was never able to hold it for any significant length of time. USAF tac air was not used to support operations in this area.[15/] (See Figure II-2 and II-3 for maps illustrating central and southern Laos.)

In southern Laos, the Bolovens Plateau campaign began with the fall of Paksong to enemy forces, in their effort to drive RLG forces further from the infiltration corridors in southern Steel Tiger. Fighting centered around Phakkout for the next month, before RLG forces fell back to defensive positions around Pakse. Early in July, friendly forces resumed the offensive, moving eastward on Route 23 toward Paksong.[16/]

On 28 July RLG forces opened a second offensive by taking Saravane and, subsequently, moving south. Enemy forces put a strong resistance around Paksong, but were forced to evacuate when RLG forces from the north advanced on the city in mid-September. For the rest of the Commando Hunt VI campaign, RLG forces controlled the areas around Paksong and Saravane, and were attempting to clear Route 23 west of Saravane as the enemy managed to keep forces near enough to disrupt friendly traffic. USAF involvement in this area was limited to occasional support of troops in contact (TICs).[17/]

Barrel Roll

In Barrel Roll, ground activity during Commando Hunt VI took place almost entirely in the vicinity of the Plaine des Jarres* (PDJ). The enemy offensive against Luang Prabang was stopped as Commando Hunt VI opened, and RLG forces began to roll the enemy forces back from there and from Long Tieng and Sam Thong.[18/] (Figure II-4, shows Barrel Roll area.)

Royal Laotian Government control of the PDJ increased until late August when an enemy offensive regained for them the northern portion of the PDJ. However, the rest of the Plain was still in friendly hands at the end of the campaign. Royal Laotian Government forces took Muong Soui on 25 September, consolidating control of Route 4/7 west of the Plain. As the campaign ended, enemy activity consisted of resupply, attacks by fire, and small-unit probes, harassing airstrips and fire support bases. This indicated that the enemy planned an offensive in the near future.[19/]

United States Air Force activity consisted of strikes against truck parks and storage areas in the PDJ and vicinity, support of TICs, and strikes against IDPs east of the PDJ. The enemy's primary supply route, 7, was interdicted through most of August and September, and occasionally in October.[20/]

---

*French for "Plain of Jars."

CENTRAL LAOS

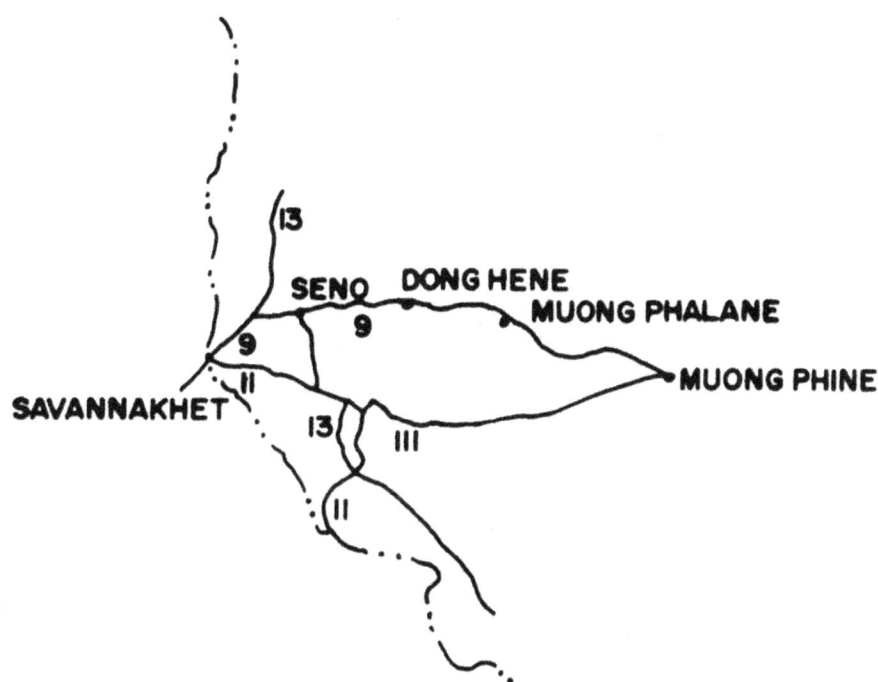

Figure II-2

SOUTHERN LAOS-BOLOVENS PLATEAU

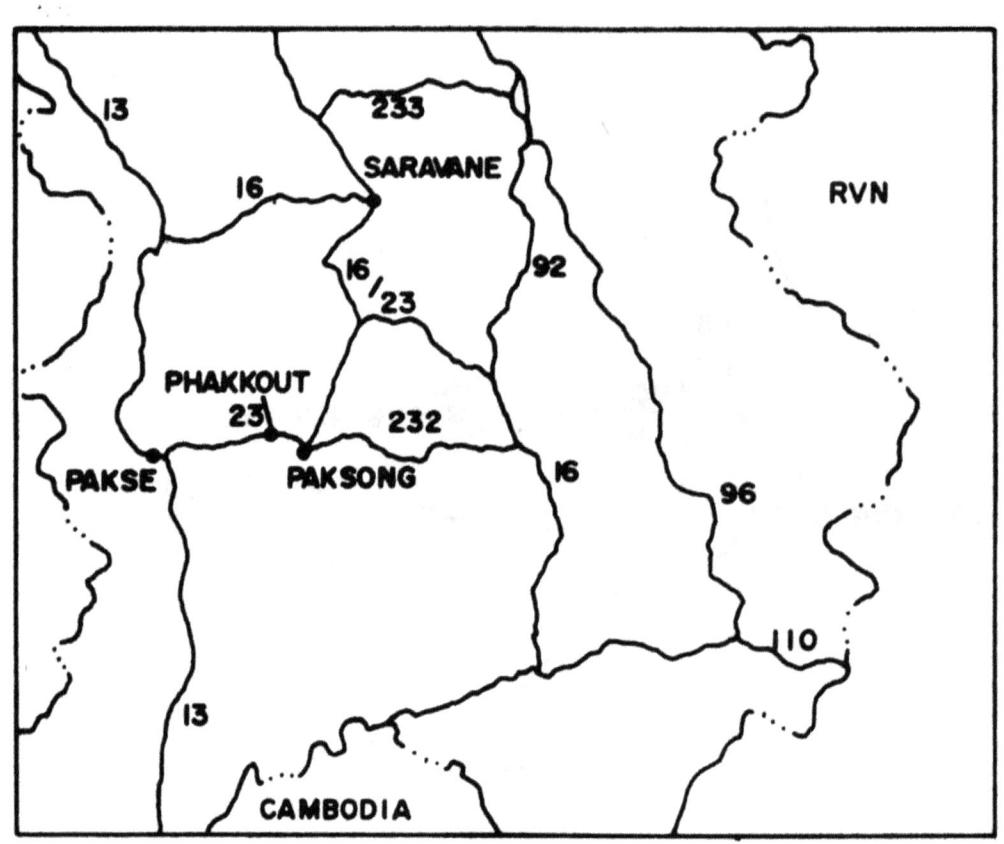

Figure II-3

Republic of Vietnam

General Activity

Enemy-initiated activity in the RVN subsided during the wet season, except for attempts to disrupt elections in August and October. These attempts failed, as the elections were held on schedule, and the incumbent, President Thieu, was re-elected handily.[21/] (See Figure II-5 for map of RVN.)

The Vietnam Air Force (VNAF) took a greater part in the air war, flying two-thirds of the attack sorties in-country, as compared to slightly less than half during Commando Hunt V.[22/]

Route 103

Photo reconnaissance early in the campaign revealed that the enemy was constructing a new road, designated Route 103, through the western Demilitarized Zone (DMZ) and into Military Region 1 (MR-1) of the RVN. The effort to extend Route 103 from NVN coincided with other construction activity by which the enemy obviously intended to establish an LOC from the DMZ to other routes near Khe Sanh. Completion of such a route structure would significantly reduce the transit time of supplies from NVN to his forces in the RVN and reduce the exposure to Allied interdiction efforts.[23/]

Extension of NVN Route 103 was initially reported by an Army L-19 pilot in May 1971. Clouds covered this area of the RVN much of the year and often prevented visual or photo reconnaissance. However, photography in June revealed construction on NVN Route 103 and on an extension south into the DMZ and the RVN. Four kilometers of completed construction on the extension were evident in June. By July this distance had doubled. Photo and visual reconnaissance detected personnel clearing ground by hand, vehicles, and bulldozer activity.[24]

During July, construction was evident at several locations along the Route 103 extension, 102B (an east-west route within the DMZ), and 120B (a route which entered the DMZ from NVN about 15 kilometers east of Route 103). By the end of July photo interpreters confirmed construction activity almost all the way from the DMZ to Route 608 in MR-1. In addition, Route 120 had been extended until it linked with Route 103, about a mile south of the DMZ.[25]

In August photo interpreters identified existing and projected route alignments as the new structure developed. The significance of the enemy activity was evident: he was working on a direct north-south LOC which would enable him to move his supplies and equipment into the RVN without entering Laos.[26]

Operations

Seventh Air Force countered enemy activity along Route 103 south of the DMZ, beginning on 9 August 1971 with five seedings segments, each 300 meters wide by 800 long, that were mined with a mixture of antipersonnel and antivehicular munitions. A typical munitions package emplaced on one seeding segment consisted of 55 dispensers (79,750 mines) of CDU-14 antipersonnel munitions (Gravel), eight dispensers

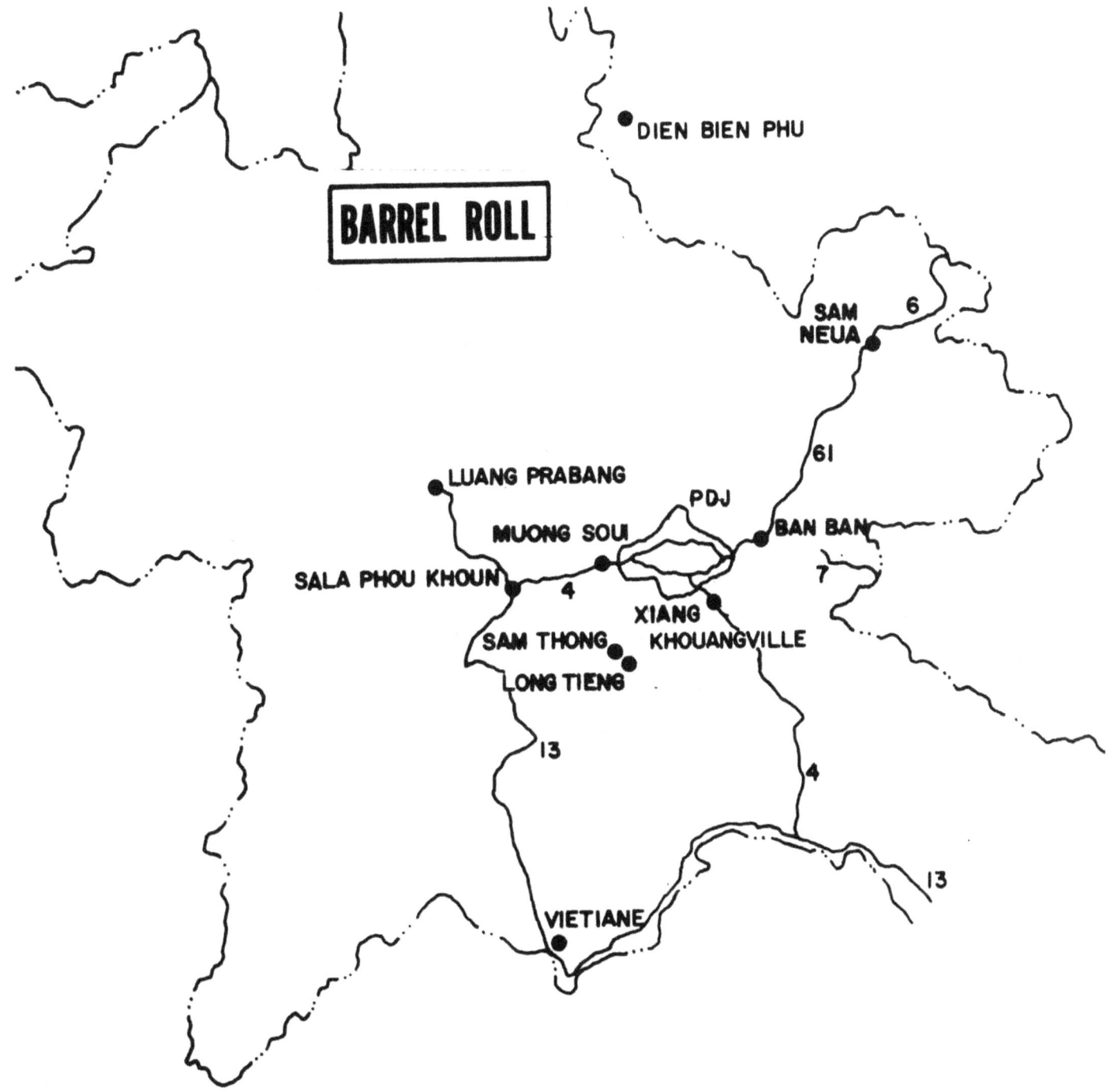

Figure II-4

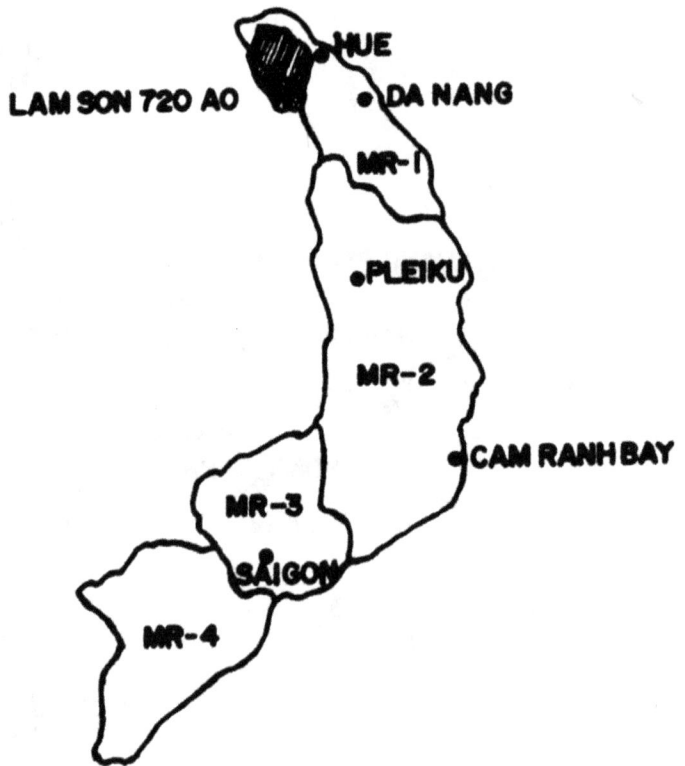

Figure II-5

(5,360 mines) of CBU-42 wide area antipersonnel mines (WAAPM), and 80 MK-36 magnetic mines.[27/]

The seedings segments were located on Route 103 or on the projected path of the road in areas under construction. Additionally, sensors were employed with each seeding segment to reveal enemy construction or clearing activity. Quick Reaction Force (QRF) aircraft were also alerted and ordered to strike enemy-initiated sensor activity. Mines were reseeded after these strikes or new seeding segments and sensors were added as they became necessary due to enemy by-passing attempts. If a particular seeding segment was not struck, but the enemy was known to be in the area, then that segment was reseeded on a regular basis determined by the time it was expected to take natural causes and the normal expiration of mines to deplete the segment.[28/] (See Figures II-6 and II-7 for the general location of the Route 103 area and for the location of seeding segments within the area.)

Segments 861, 862, 863, and 865 were seeded on 9 August. Initial seeding dates of other segments were: 864, 11 Aug; 871, 16 Aug; 867, 25 Aug; and 868, 26 Aug.[29/]

Level of Effort, and Evaluation of Results

Altogether, 473 strike sorties were flown against Route 103, expending 3,272 weapons. Of these, 285 sorties expended 1,823 weapons of the types named above as being in a munitions package. The majority of these sorties, and of all strike sorties, were flown before 31 August. Also, the majority of these weapons, and of all weapons, were expended by 31 August. The majority of the sorties flown, and of the weapons expended, were against the three northernmost seeding segments, 865, 867, and 868.[30]

The number of enemy-initiated sensor activations varied from week to week, from a high of 33 from 22 through 28 September, to a low of zero from 8 through 14 September, and from 20 October on. Of the activations to which QRF aircraft responded, the average time from initial sensor activation through assessment, launch command, scramble, and arrival over target was 63 minutes.[31]

Photo reconnaissance on 29 July showed the enemy to have completed 20 kilometers of road. By 23 August that figure reached 25 km, and was increased to 26 km on 5 September. After 26 September, when the figure had reached 26.9 km, no further construction was observed.[32]

Although air power did not completely halt the enemy's construction activity, intelligence sources indicated that he was forced to delay his timetable and build numerous by-passes, and that the morale of his construction troops was affected by the continued application of US air resources. This information and the enemy's intent, demonstrated by his preservance in continuing construction despite U.S. air attacks, gives an indication of the emphasis which he placed on Route 103. By mid-November 1971, the construction on Route 103 had halted, because of a combination of the onset of the rainy season and the success of the air effort.[33]

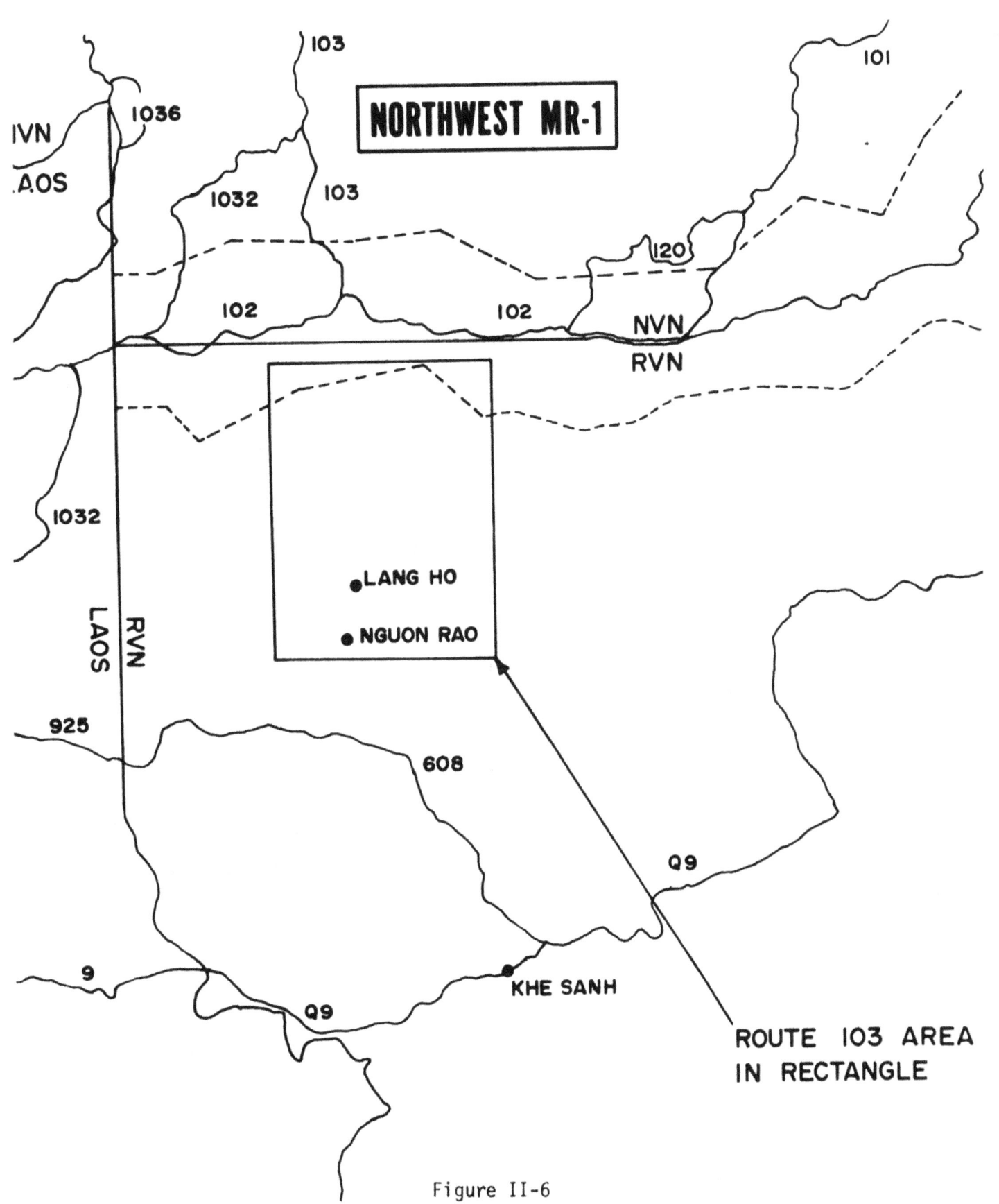

Figure II-6

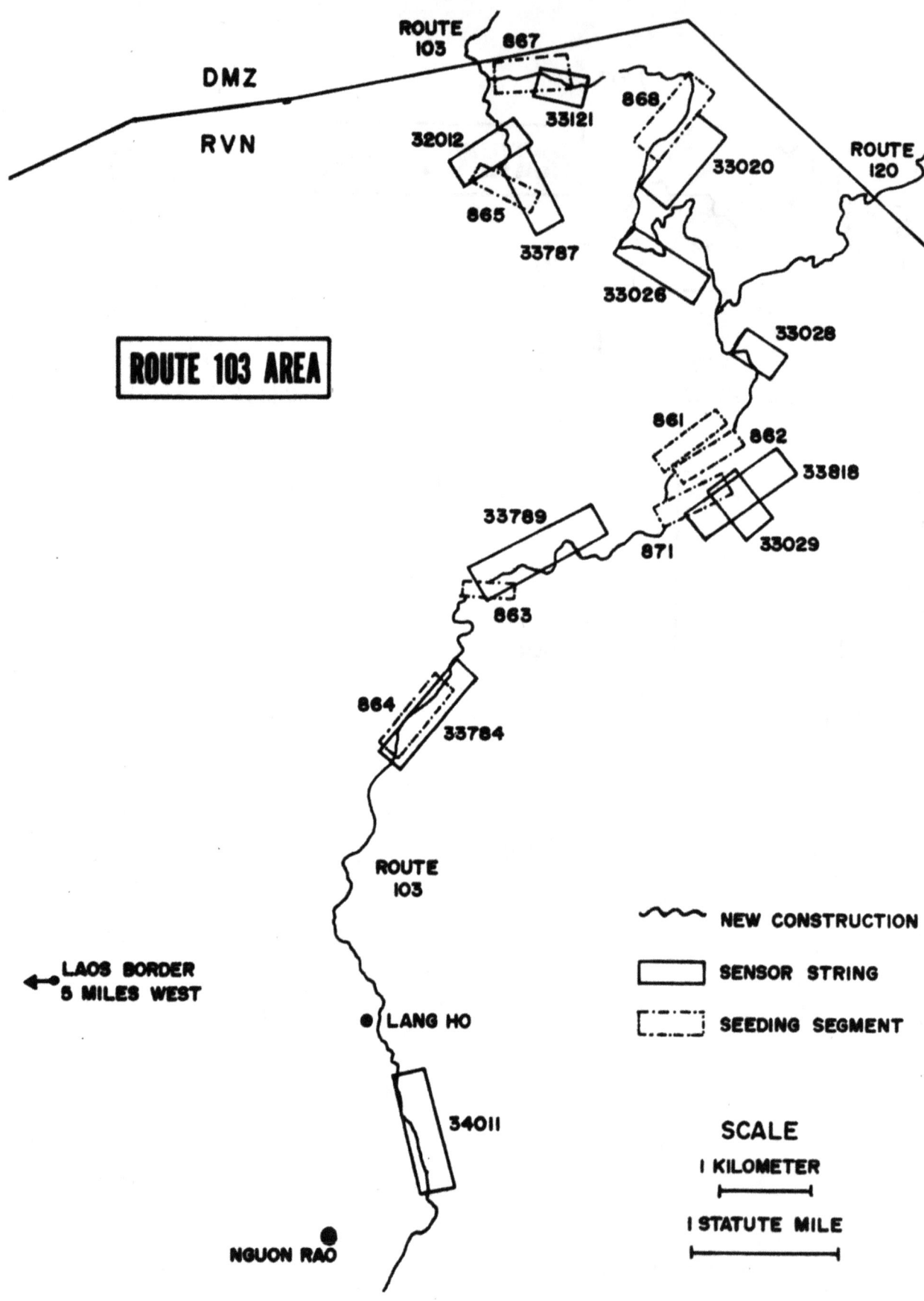

Figure II-7

Cambodia

Activity in Cambodia consisted of Army of the Republic of Vietnam (ARVN) and Forces Armees Nationales Khmer* (FANK) operations in MR-1 and MR-2, and FANK operations in MR-3 and MR-4. The ARVN withdrew from Cambodian territory in late May, but returned soon thereafter. The FANK mounted a highly successful operation in June and July, denying the enemy the use of the Tonle Toch River. They were able to keep Pich Nil Pass open for all but the last week of the wet season. Convoys from Battambang and Kompong Som, and up the Mekong River, reached Phnom Penh with only brief interruptions. Late in the season, FANK forces were able to open Route 6 to Kompong Thom briefly, but the enemy mounted an offensive that brought much of Route 6 under attack, and cut it north and south of Rumlong, just before the end of the period. The enemy held MR-5 throughout the season, except for a brief ARVN maneuver which reached Snoul in late May. [34/] (See Figure II-8 for map of Cambodia.)

*French for "Cambodian National Armed Forces."

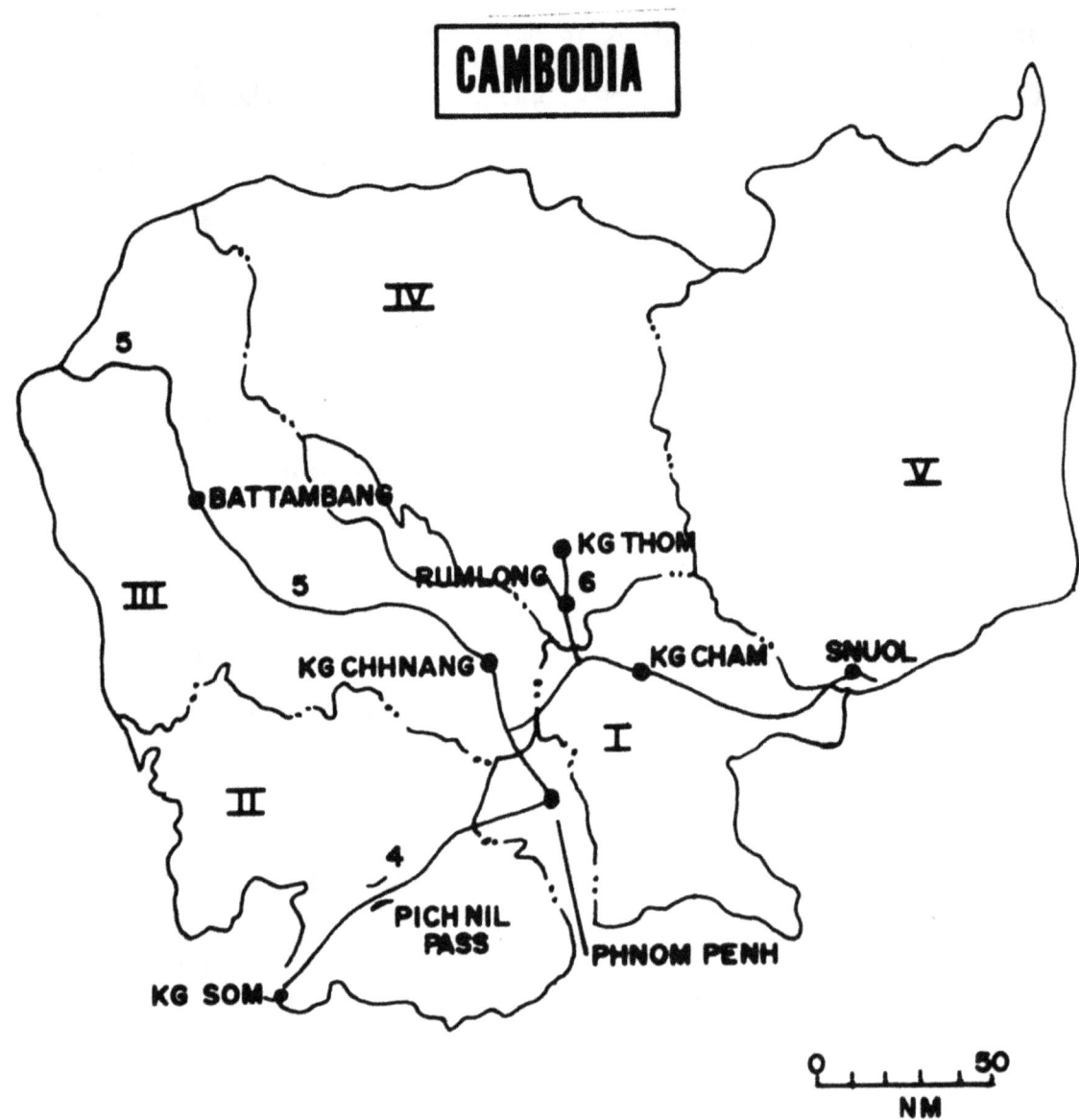

Figure II-8

CHAPTER III

CAMPAIGN RESULTS IN STEEL TIGER

The Effort Against Trucks

It was expected that the number of trucks moving in Steel Tiger would decrease as the rains degraded the LOCs. However, trucks were still considered prime targets, to be struck whenever they could be found. The weight of effort against trucks was to be commensurate with enemy truck activities.[35]

Resources

The specialized systems for attacking trucks at night were the AC-130 and AC-119K gunships, and B-57Gs. Because the AC-130s and AC-119Ks lacked flak-suppression capability, they required fighter escorts when operating in high-threat areas. Nearly all fighters and attack aircraft attacked trucks to varying degrees; they were the only systems used to strike during daylight.[36]

AC-130

The AC-130 gunship force for this campaign was smaller than in the dry season campaign. The Surprise Package aircraft was available throughout the campaign. The Update AC-130s were returned to the United States for modification to the Pave Pronto configuration, which included installation of an improved low-light-level television, a sensor slaving unit, and a fire control officer console.[37] There were eight or nine AC-130s available for most of the campaign, but that figure rose to 12 by the end of October with the return of the Pave Prontos.[38]

With the exception of the areas within 20 nautical miles of the Mu Gia and Ban Karai Passes, which were sometimes confirmed Surface-to-Air Missile (SAM) operating areas, AC-130s were not restricted from operating anywhere in Steel Tiger by the AAA threat.[39/]

AC-119K

Through the wet season there were 10 to 12 AC-119Ks in SEA.[40/] They were restricted from flying within 20 nautical miles of the input passes, and in the high-threat area around Tchepone. Because of the Tchepone threat, AC-119Ks were not fragged to VR Sector 4.[41/]

B-57G

There were nine or ten B-57Gs available throughout the campaign.[42/] Their primary weapons against trucks were M-36E2 incendiary clusters and laser-guided MK-82 bombs.[43/] However, as trucks became more difficult to find in July through October, B-57Gs struck truck parks and storage areas more often than trucks.[44/]

The low B-57 sortie rate in July through September was due to the removal, modification, and replacement of the AN/APQ-130 forward-looking radar. During modification, the B-57Gs did not fly in Steel Tiger. The modification improved the radar picture, and increased the maximum usable range. It was also intended that the previously ineffective ground-moving-target indicator be made effective, but results during the remainder of the campaign were inconclusive.[45/]

While the normal B-57G role was basically a self-FAC effort, crews also responded to advisories from Task Force Alpha (TFA) and FAC aircraft and worked as a team with the AC-130 gunships.[46/]

Truck Movements

The number of sensor-detected truck movements in Steel Tiger, which was already decreasing weekly as the dry season ended, continued to do so dramatically. There was a brief surge in late June and early July when the weather cleared, but shortly thereafter the number of detections dropped below 200 per week, and remained there through the rest of the campaign.[47/]

The number of Igloo White sensor-detected truck movements, while not a precise indicator of the absolute level of truck activity, or of the number of potential targets, was the best available measure and was therefore used for planning; however, the number of active sensor strings varied from a high of 117 during the week of 23 through 29 June to a low of 50 during the week of 29 September through 5 October.[48/] While these changes did affect trends in sensor detections, the field strength did not change at as great a rate as did the level of sensor-detected truck movements; hence the general decrease and later increase in that level reflected real changes in truck activity. Also, while sensors were not generally monitored during the day, selective monitoring indicated that truck movement then was negligible.[49/] Despite heavy continued presence of FACs and strike aircraft, visual observations of moving trucks were much lower in the daytime than at night. There were 5361 trucks observed during the campaign, 3,354 of them at night. Only 1,774 of the 5,361 trucks were observed to be moving.[50] A possible interpretation of the high proportion of parked trucks observed was that they were involved in the enemy's road-repair effort.

Another indication of the decrease of truck movement through the campaign was the weight of effort against trucks. The weekly numbers of combat sorties flown and of combat sorties striking trucks decreased steadily through Commando Hunt VI. The proportion striking trucks was over 20 percent through May, over 10 percent through June, and below or just barely above 10 percent each week thereafter.[51]

Force Effectiveness

Trends in trucks observed, struck, and destroyed or damaged are shown in Figure III-1. The trends tended to behave similarly, with a few minor exceptions.[52]

Figure III-2, shows three indicative ratios of the quantities graphed in Figure III-1. The first is the ratio of trucks struck per truck observed, which shows a downward trend over the campaign. This can be accounted for by the deterioration of weather in Steel Tiger and the replacement of experienced crews by new ones. For the entire season, the ratio was 71.4 percent.[53]

The second ratio is that of trucks destroyed or damaged to those struck. The ratio fluctuated widely, and could not be described as having a trend. Over the campaign, the ratio was 53 percent, somewhat

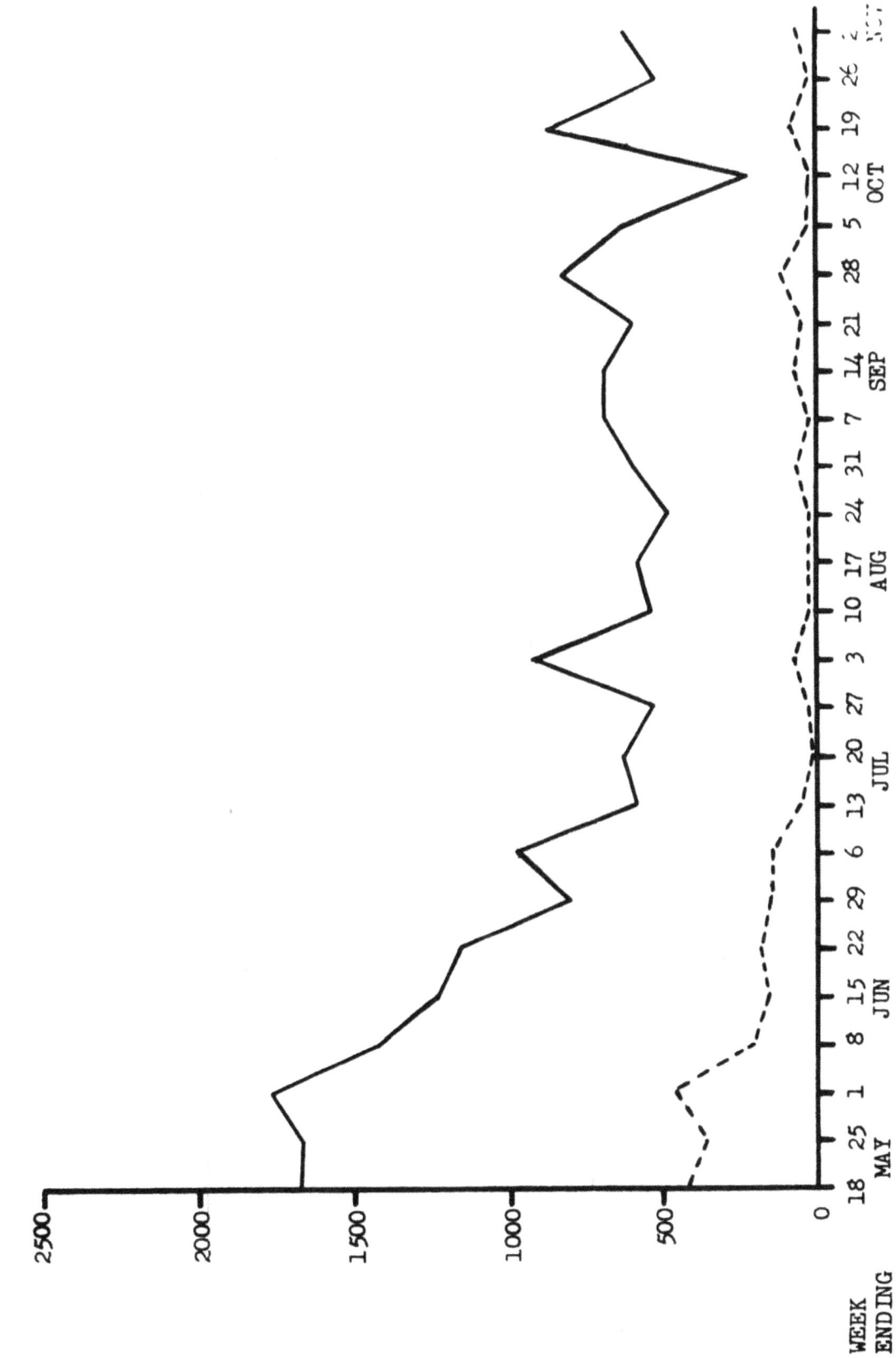

FIGURE III-1
TOTAL SORTIES AND SORTIES STRIKING TRUCKS

FIGURE III-2a
TRUCKS STRUCK PER TRUCK OBSERVED

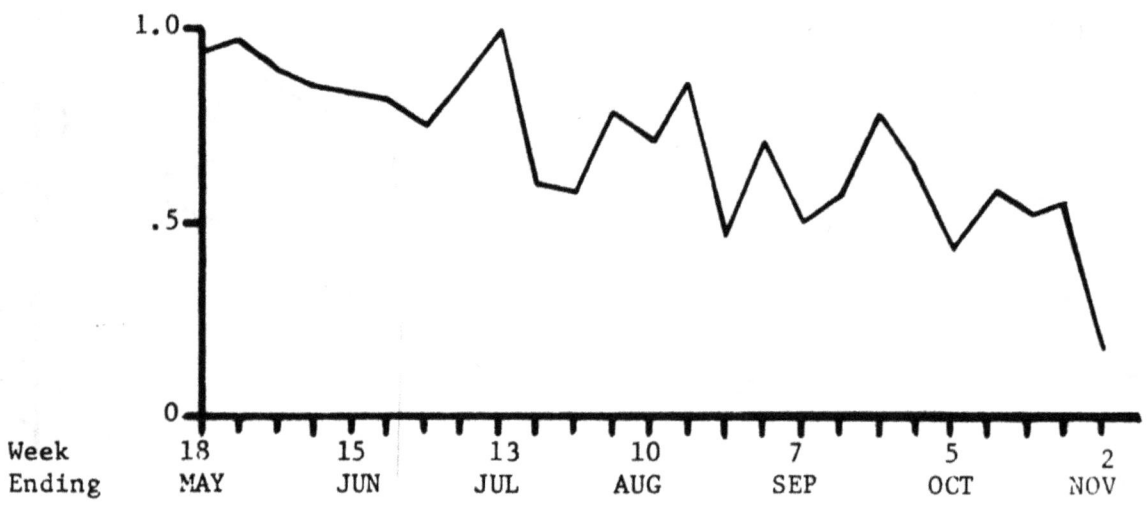

FIGURE III-2b
TRUCKS DESTROYED OR DAMAGED PER TRUCK STRUCK

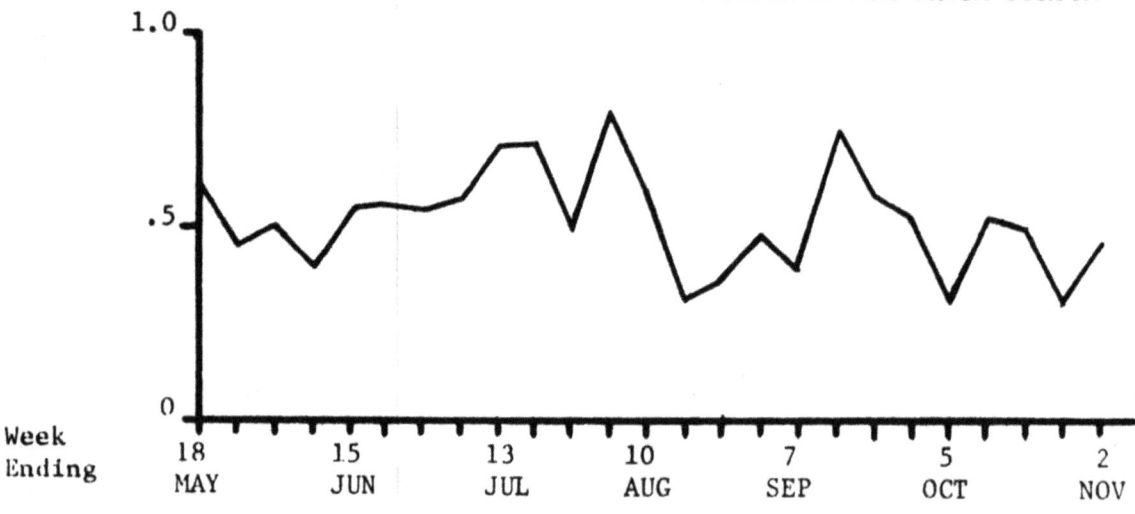

FIGURE III-2c
TRUCKS DESTROYED OR DAMAGED PER TRUCK OBSERVED

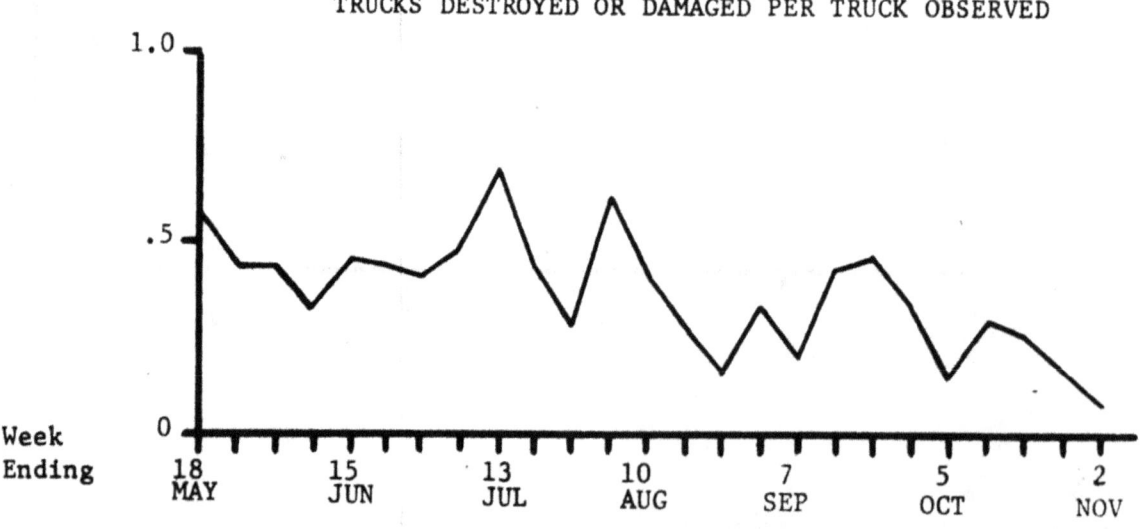

lower than the 64 percent recorded during Commando Hunt V.[54]

The third ratio is a useful measure of force performance, the percentage of observed trucks that were destroyed or damaged, which is the product of the factors just discussed. The downward trend was just the opposite of that experienced in the preceding dry season.[55]

Table III-1, summarizes overall force performance against trucks. These data include sorties reporting results not observable (RNO). Approximately one-quarter of all sorties fell in that category during Commando Hunt VI.[56]

The capability to assess strike results by aircraft on the scene depended on a variety of factors. FACs were in a better position to observe strike results than jet aircraft crews flying higher and faster. Weather, darkness, smoke, and foliage also affected visibility. The gunship crews were assisted by electronic observation devices, but their capability varied. Observation was also affected in many cases by the need to evade AAA firing.

Bomb Damage Assessment (BDA) Criteria

The criteria for assessing strike results depended on the weapon system and observation techniques involved. These criteria had to be uncomplicated and compatible with the degree of observable detail. The criteria for a destroyed truck for an aircraft attacking with bombs were that the truck be one or more of the following:[57]

1. No longer visible after a direct hit.

2. Observed to be aflame.

3. Observed to be a mass of twisted metal after a strike, or

4. Rendered unusable and irreparable after a strike.

For a damaged truck, the criteria were that the truck:[58]

1. Have parts missing, such as the hood, fenders, wheels, or portions of the undercarriage.

2. Be stopped and obviously unable to continue after the strike, or

3. Be overturned with no fire or explosion.

There were two sets of criteria for the gunships because of differences in armament. For both 40mm and 20mm guns, a truck was considered destroyed if it was observed to have exploded or burned after projectile impact. A truck was considered damaged if it received a direct impact of a 40mm projectile; however, a 20mm impact was not considered to have damaged the truck unless it stopped and was not observed to move again.[59]

Significance of Results

Attempts to quantify the impact of truck losses upon the enemy were hampered by a lack of definite information on the enemy's capability and intent. However, if he could be assumed to have intended an early major effort in the following dry season, his failure, and therefore, the success of the interdiction program, could be inferred from a comparison of sensor-detected movements over the first four

FORCE PERFORMANCE AGAINST TRUCKS

	15-31 May	Jun	Jul	Aug	Sep	Oct	Total
Total Sorties Flown	4257	5090	3011	2688	3071	2680	20797
Sorties Striking Trucks	972	767	256	160	259	211	2625
% Sorties Striking Trucks	22.8	15.1	8.5	6.0	8.4	7.9	12.6
Trucks Struck	1948	1015	477	187	359	193	4179
Trucks Destroyed or Damaged (D/D)	983	538	257	99	208	84	2169
Trucks D/D per Sorties Striking Trucks	1.01	.70	1.00	.62	.80	.40	.83
Trucks D/D per Truck Struck	.50	.53	.54	.53	.58	.43	.52

weeks of the Commando Hunt VII campaign, and the same calendar weeks of the Commando Hunt V campaign. The figures for each of the four pairs of weeks showed a greater number of detections during Commando Hunt V. For the four weeks combined, the Commando Hunt VII figure was 28 percent less. This measure, at least, marked the campaign as a success.[60/]

The primary measure of effectiveness for recent interdiction campaigns has been the amount of supplies which exited Steel Tiger into Cambodia and the RVN. (Commando Hunt VI input and throughput figures are given in Appendix B.) The number of trucks destroyed or damaged had been a measure of the accomplishment of the usual secondary objective, that of increasing the enemy's cost of moving supplies. Its most constructive use had been in determining the relative effectiveness of weapons systems, for the purpose of allocating air resources during the campaign. For this purpose, the combined figure of destroyed and damaged trucks, reported on the basis of consistent criteria, was an adequate index.

Aircraft Effectiveness

Performance data for individual aircraft systems are shown in Table III-2. The AC-130 was the only system that struck trucks on more than one-half of its sorties in Steel Tiger. For the three special systems combined, the figure was 48 percent. Among the special systems, the AC-119Ks did better in terms of trucks destroyed or damaged per sortie striking trucks than the AC-130s, which in turn did better than the B-57Gs.[61/]

TABLE III-2

AIRCRAFT PERFORMANCE AGAINST TRUCKS

	F-4	A-6	A-7	AC-119	AC-130	B-57
Total Sorties Flown	9731	1381	6620	258	402	403
Sorties Striking Trucks	1361	74	655	115	273	123
% Sorties Striking Trucks	14.0	5.4	9.9	44.6	67.8	30.5
Trucks Struck	1693	70	550	444	1096	235
Trucks D/D	650	24	312	338	683	125
Trucks D/D per Sortie Striking Trucks	.48	.32	.48	2.94	2.50	1.02
Trucks D/D per Truck Struck	.38	.34	.57	.75	.62	.31

Of the fighter-attack aircraft, both the F-4 and the A-7 destroyed or damaged more trucks per sortie striking trucks than they had during the dry season. F-4s totalled more sorties striking trucks and more trucks struck than any other aircraft. Consequently, F-4s destroyed or damaged the second highest number of trucks of any aircraft type. [62/]

Of the other aircraft that struck trucks during the dry season, the A-4 failed to strike a truck during the wet season, while the thirteen A-1 sorties that struck trucks destroyed or damaged five. Before the F-100 left SEA in June, 50 sorties struck trucks, destroying or damaging thirty. [63/]

The decrease from the dry-season campaign in trucks destroyed or damaged per sortie for special systems could be accounted for by the decrease in trucks available. This did not affect the figure for fighter aircraft, which tended to make only one or two strikes per sortie. If trucks were harder to find, they would simply take longer to look for them. The trend in trucks destroyed or damaged per sortie striking trucks for the entire force was downward, reflecting worsening weather and decreasing enemy activity. [64/]

Effort Against Other Targets

In addition to trucks, air forces struck a variety of other targets to interdict the enemy's total logistic system in Laos. Sixty-five percent of the tac air strike sorties during Commando Hunt VI attacked targets within three major categories: truck parks and storage areas, AAA/SAM defenses, and LOCs. Fighter and attack aircraft made almost all these attacks, but gunships and B-57Gs struck these targets on occasions.[65/]

Arc Light cells also struck truck parks and storage and LOCs. Because of the size of a B-52 cell's bomb pattern, it sometimes included both target types. Those sorties that struck some storage facilities are included here under truck parks and storage areas.

Truck Parks and Storage Areas

The enemy reacted to air interdiction during previous campaigns by developing a well-dispersed complex of well-camouflaged truck parks and storage areas. This complex handled the supplies moving through his logistics system; it also supported construction, operation, and maintenance of the road network. The typical truck park was located under jungle canopy 200 to 300 meters off a main road and near a water source. Trucks were parked in clusters of two or three, 20 to 30 meters apart, sometimes in excavated inclined trenches.[66/]

The heavy tree cover and camouflage made detection of storage areas difficult and hampered assessment of strike results. Fifty-six percent of tac air strikes against such targets reported RNO. Most of the observed results were fires and secondary explosions.[67/]

Probing strikes were often launched against suspected truck parks and storage areas. Most of these strikes produced no results, but when secondary fires and explosions were observed, revealing that either munitions or flammable supplies were present, additional sorties were flown against the target to take advantage of the discovery.

There were no targets in the thousand-fires-and-explosions class reported, as there were during Commando Hunt V. Weather not only decreased the amount of bombing against targets in areas where only strikes under visual meteorological conditions were permitted, but also decreased the probability of observing results on a probing strike.

Several B-57 strikes against TFA-developed targets in late June yielded as many as 45 fires and secondary explosions. On 25 August, a series of seven F-4s and four A-7s struck a storage area along Route 9222, reporting 54 secondary explosions. On 20 September, six F-4s and eight A-7s struck a target on Route 96, reporting 11 fires and 20 medium and 207 small secondary explosions, the greatest number reported from a single target during Commando Hunt VI. The last significant strike of the campaign took place on 25 October east of Saravane, where 15 Navy aircraft reported 19 secondary explosions, a truck destroyed, and a truc and a jeep damaged. There were large variations in the tactical air effort against truck parks and storage areas in Steel Tiger, but about 26 percent of the sorties flown struck these targets. The ratio of fires and secondary explosions per tac air sortie against truck parks and storage areas ranged from a low of .21 in July to a high of 1.73 in September. The low June and July figures corresponded to the period of greatest cloud cover.[68/]

Results for Arc Light sorties against targets, including stored supplies, are only approximations, since B-52 bombing altitudes, often above cloud layers, precluded accurate assessment of results. Over the campaign 56 percent of the Arc Light sorties reported RNO.[69]

Air forces, other than Arc Light, recorded a total of 9,608 fires and secondary explosions. Of these, 1,978 were associated with the destruction of trucks. The difference, 7,630 fires and explosions, may be a better indication of the total damage inflicted upon the enemy's stored supplies. In addition, because of the heavy foliage covering most of the storage areas, damage to nonflammable supplies was seldom recorded; therefore, total damage to the enemy logistics system was probably higher than the statistics indicate.[70]

Effort Against Enemy Defenses

The cost to the enemy in terms of equipment destroyed or damaged and additional supply requirements represented but a partial measure of the effectiveness of attacks against defenses. The most important effect of these attacks was to keep the threat environment at a level that allowed other strike resources to conduct an effective campaign against the enemy logistic system. Enemy defenses caused 35 hits including seven losses, compared to 44 hits and 13 losses for the previous wet season.

Attacks Against AAA

AAA positions were well-fortified and difficult to destroy, although laser-guided bombs (LGBs) could accomplish their destruction. However, area weapons (CBU-24, CBU-49, M-36E2, and napalm) were able to silence a gun by causing the crew to take cover, which usually kept it from firing again for some time. Fighters employed such weapons to suppress flak for gunships. Sorties and results against AAA in Steel Tiger included 904 strikes, destroying or damaging 231 gun positions. 72/

Attacks Against Surface-to-Air Missiles

There were 10 SAM firings observed, none of which caused aircraft loss or damage. However, two Buffalo Hunter drones were believed to have been shot down by SAMs. All firings were from NVN, where the enemy maintained an average of 31 occupied and 167 unoccupied SAM sites, with little variation in those numbers. The few sites discovered in Laos remained unoccupied during the campaign, although a missile transporter was sighted and struck on Route 1036D west of the DMZ and destroyed. Heavy canopy prevented reconnaissance efforts from determining whether the transporter had been carrying a SAM. 73/

There were eight firings of air-to-ground missiles against NVN radars during the campaign. A successful firing probably occurred on 22 May when a Shrike AGM-45 was fired at a FAN SONG radar operating along Route 15C, about 20 miles north of Mu Gia Pass, and detonated on the ground just as the radar went off the air. Of the other firings, one failed to guide (at the same target as above), one was not observed to ignite after launching, and the results of the other five were not observed. 74/

Protective-Reaction Strikes

Protective-reaction strikes in North Vietnam had three basic objectives:

1. To provide a realistic deterrent to enemy activity in NVN which was a direct threat to the safety of allied air operations in Laos, RVN, and NVN;

2. To destroy enemy equipment which could be used in carrying out that threat; and

3. To demonstrate to the North Vietnamese that North Vietnam was not a total sanctuary within which all hostile activity could escape Allied attention. [75]

The majority of the protective-reaction strikes were conducted by reconnaissance escorts against enemy positions firing on the reconnaissance aircraft or by F-105G SAM-suppression aircraft. [76] One major preplanned protective-reaction operation requiring higher headquarters approval was conducted during Commando Hunt VI: Prize Bull.

At the direction of the Joint Chiefs of Staff, Prize Bull was executed on 21 September. The program was scheduled in three waves; however, the third was cancelled due to poor target weather. The 196 aircraft that flew struck three Petroleum, Oil, and Lubricant (POL) storage areas, destroying an estimated 470,000 gallons of storage capacity, and starting several fires that lasted two days or more. Poor weather hampered bomb damage assessment on all three targets. [77]

Effort Against Lines of Communication

During the wet season, the enemy was expected to retain road repair and construction capability in Steel Tiger. The principal effort against LOCs was planned to be against road construction activities, and against the IDPs throughout Steel Tiger where geographical features and the effects of the rains would tend to make repair difficult and time-consuming to the enemy. While not a conclusive measurement of the impact of LOC interdiction on the enemy, the number of cuts and slides (3,663 by 7,239 sorties) was an indirect indication of the price the enemy had to pay to maintain his road system. For comparison, 10,340 Tac Air sorties struck LOCs in Steel Tiger during Commando Hunt V, resulting in 4513 cuts and slides.[78/]

Like the data on Arc Light sorties against truck park and storage areas, the results of Arc Light sorties against LOCs were crude approximations. Over the campaign, 49 percent of the Arc Light sorties flown against LOCs reported RNO. This percentage ranged from 35 for May to 64 for June, reflecting the worsening of the weather over those two months.[79/]

Overall Assessment

Of the 4,753 tons of supplies the enemy brought into Steel Tiger from NVN, 1,406 tons, or 30 percent, reached RVN or Cambodia.[80/] This throughput-to-input ratio for Commando Hunt VI was one to three as compared to the 1970 wet season campaign, when the enemy put through 2,357 tons out of an input of 13,287, or 18 percent.[81/] However, the start which the enemy made in the ensuing dry season was somewhat slower than in 1970, in spite of his increased roadbuilding effort.[82/] In this respect, Commando Hunt VI was a success.

FOOTNOTES*

CHAPTER I

1. (TS) Seventh Air Force Operation Plan 730, Southwest Monsoon Campaign (7AF OPLAN 730), 22 September 1971.

2. Ibid.

3. Ibid.

4. Ibid. Also, (S) Commando Hunt V, Headquarters Seventh Air Force, May 1971.

5. (S) Commando Hunt V. Also, (TS) Message, Subject: Air Activity Level for FY 72 and FY 73, COMUSMACV, 220630 May 1971.

6. (TS) 7AF Oplan 730.

7. (S) Message, subj: Southwest Monsoon Plan, COMUSMACV, 240810Z May 1971. Also, (TS) Message, Subj: 7AF Oplan 730, CINCPACAF 171838Z May 1971.

8. (S) Commando Hunt V, Chapter VIII.

CHAPTER II

9. (S) Commando Hunt V.

10. (S) Study by the author of Seventh Air Force Weekly Air Intelligence Summaries covering the period May through October 1971 (WAIS Study).

11. Ibid.

12. (S) Message, Subj: Steel Tiger VR Sectors, 7AF(DO), 180330Z June 1971.

13. (S) WAIS Study.

14. (S) WAIS, 6 November 1971.

15. (S) WAIS Study.

*All portions extracted from TS documents are of SECRET or lower classification.

16. Ibid.

17. Ibid.

18. Ibid.

19. Ibid.

20. Ibid.

21. Ibid.

22. Ibid. Also, (S) Commando Hunt V.

23. (S) Route 103 Briefing, 7AF (INTSA) Working Paper, undated.

24. Ibid.

25. Ibid.

26. Ibid.

27. Ibid. Also, (C) Joint Munitions Effectiveness Manual, Weapons Characteristics, 10 March 1969. Published under auspices of
28. JCS by activities of all services. USAF OPR: OCAMA (MMSU), Tinker AFB, Oklahoma.

28. Ibid.

29. Compiled from (S) 7AF Daily Fragmentary Orders and (S) Southeast Asia Data Base (SEADAB).

30. (S) SEADAB.

31. (C) Blue Chip/Igloo White Log, 7AF (DOCP).

32. Interview of Capt J. D. Henderson, 7AF (DOA) action officer, Route 103, March 1972.

33. (S) Route 103 Briefing. Also, (S) Photo Intelligence Brief #6112/6..7, 7AF (12RITS), 19 November 1971.

34. WAIS Study.

CHAPTER III

35. (TS) 7AF Oplan 730.

36. (S) Commando Hunt V.

37. _Ibid_. Also, (S) Letter from 7AF (DOXFG), Subj: Commando Hunt Data Requirements on IRAN of Gunships, dated 14 February 1972.

38. (S) Command Status Book, published monthly by 7AF (ACM)(CSB).

39. Interview by author with Lt Col Donald D. Mueller, 7AF (DOA) action officer, gunship operations.

40. (S) CSB.

41. Interview with Lt Col Mueller.

42. (S) CSB.

43. (C) 7AF(DOA) Briefing to General Brown, subj: Employment of the B-57G Self-Contained Night Attack System, January 1972.

44. (S) Study by the author of weekly Igloo White OPREP-5s, published by 7AF (DOYR) (OPREP-5 Study).

45. (C) 7AF (DOA) Briefing to General Brown (See Note 9).

46. Interview with Capt Michael G. Fahey, 7AF (DOA) action officer, B-57G operations.

47. (S) OPREP-5 Study.

48. _Ibid_.

49. (S) WAIS Study.

50. (S) OPREP-5 Study.

51. _Ibid_.

52. (S) WAIS Study.

53. _Ibid_.

43

54.   <u>Ibid</u>. Also, (S) Commando Hunt V, Chapter III.

55.   <u>Ibid</u>.

56.   <u>Ibid</u>. Also, (S) Study by the author of weekly Operations Summary Briefings, 7AF (DOA), May through October 1971 (Weekly Briefing Study).

57. (S) Commando Hunt V, Chapter III.

58.   <u>Ibid</u>.

59.   <u>Ibid</u>.

60. (S) Study by the author of weekly Operations Summary Briefings, 7AF (DOA), November 1970 and November 1971 (Weekly Briefing Study - November).

61. (S) OPREP-5 Study.

62.   <u>Ibid</u>.

63.   <u>Ibid</u>.

64.   <u>Ibid</u>.

65.   <u>Ibid</u>.

66. (S) Commando Hunt V.

67. (S) OPREP-5 Study. Also, (S) Weekly Briefing Study.

68.   <u>Ibid</u>.

69. (S) WAIS Study.

70. (S) OPREP-5 Study.

71. (S) 7AF (DOY) Hit and Loss File.

72. (S) OPREP-5 Study.

73. (S) WAIS Study.

74.   <u>Ibid</u>.

75. (S) Commando Hunt V, Chapter V.

76. (S) WAIS Study.

77. (C) Talking Paper, Subj: Operation Prize Bull, 7AF (INTTC), undated.

78. (S) Commando Hunt V, Appendix A.

79. (S) WAIS Study.

80. <u>Ibid</u>.

81. (S) Infiltration Surveillance Center Data Base, TFA.

82. (S) Weekly Briefing Study--November.

APPENDIX A

AIR RESOURCES

Strike Aircraft

Table A-1 shows the number of strike aircraft possessed at each base in Thailand by month during the campaign. USAF resources located at Thai bases flew most of the sorties in Laos. (Figure A-1, on the following page, shows the location of USAF bases in SEA.)

Table A-2 shows the number of strike aircraft possessed at each base in the RVN by month. Seventh Air Force strike resources based in the RVN contributed to the dry-season campaign in Laos. The VNAF provided most of the close support required by RVN Armed Forces in the RVN and Cambodia.

Sorties

United States aircraft flew most of their sorties in Steel Tiger. Table A-3 presents sortie distribution and shows total sorties flown, whether or not ordnance was expended.

Table A-4 shows the results of U.S. air strikes in Steel Tiger.

Table A-5 shows target types struck by U.S. aircraft in Steel Tiger on their first strike.

Tables A-6 through A-13 break down the sorties flown in Steel Tiger by the different U.S. strike aircraft by target type and by month. Tables A-14 through A-17 show like data for sorties flown in Barrel Roll. When sorties struck two types of targets, they were counted by the first type struck.

Table A-18 shows the sortie rates for USAF units possessing strike aircraft.

Hits and Losses from Enemy Defenses

The numbers of USAF fixed-wing aircraft hit by and lost to enemy defenses were somewhat lower than during the previous wet season campaign. Table A-19 shows the USAF hit and loss experience in Steel Tiger and Barrel Roll. Isolated incidents account for all the fluctuation in the data.

The F-4 was the most frequently hit aircraft type, with 22 hits (two losses) in Steel Tiger and 14 hits (two losses) in Barrel Roll. Of these hits, 20 (one loss) were sustained by aircraft flying strike sorties.

Other Aircraft

Table A-20 shows the number of FAC aircraft possessed, by base and aircraft type, as of the end of the month. Table A-21 shows the same information about reconnaissance aircraft. In both tables, the numbers decreased from April to August, reflecting the phaseout of units in SEA and the return of aircraft to the U.S., or their turnover to the VNAF.

Table A-22 shows the number of FAC sorties flown by geographical area and aircraft type.

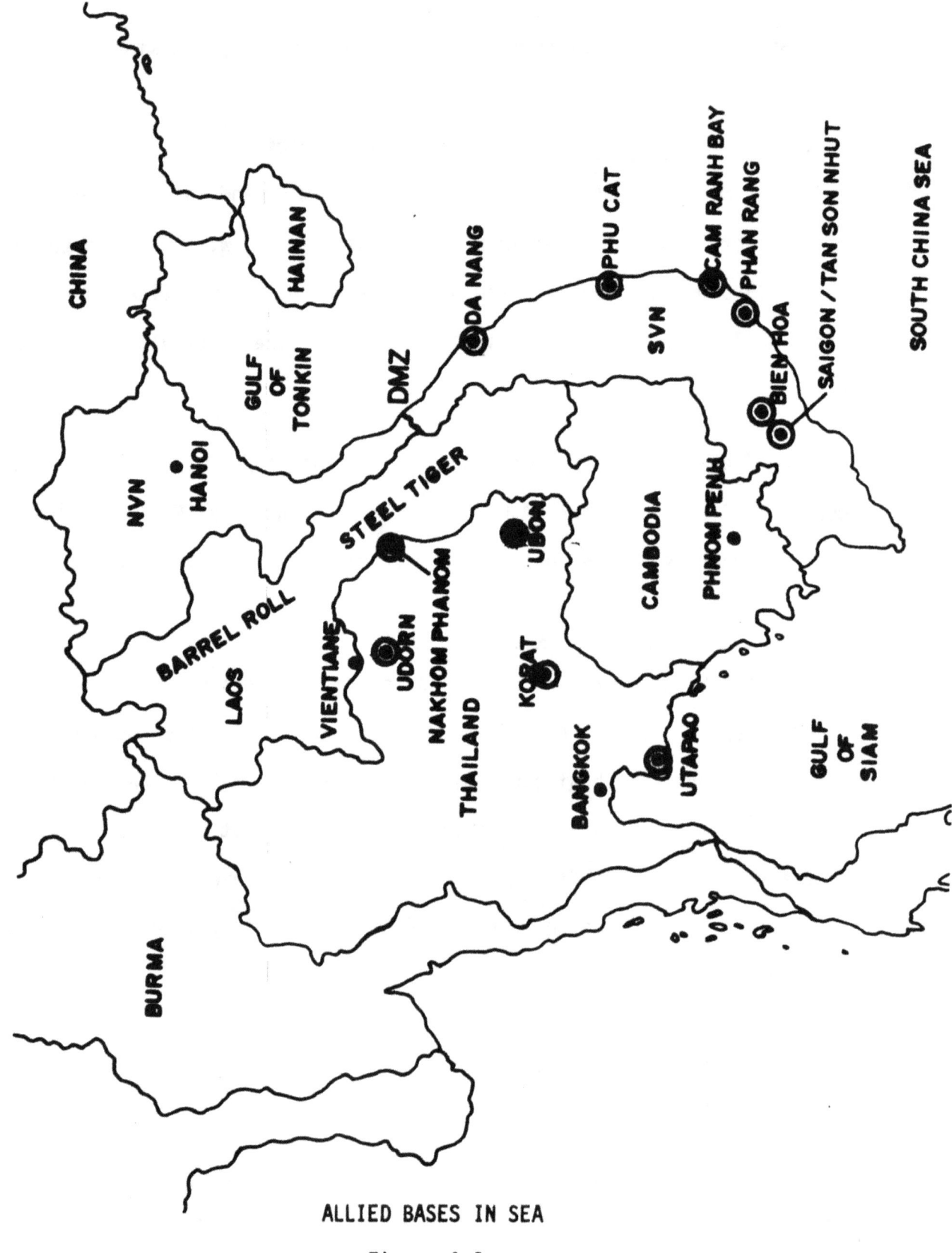

ALLIED BASES IN SEA

Figure A-1

TABLE A-1

USAF STRIKE RESOURCES IN THAILAND, AS OF END OF MONTH

	Apr	May	Jun	Jul	Aug	Sep	Oct
Nakhon Phanom							
AC-119K	6	5	7	5	16	3	9
A-1E/G/H/J	23	25	23	24	24	18	6
Korat							
F-105G	17	15	12	13	12	11	12
F-4E	32	31	34	35	36	35	35
Ubon							
A-1J	1	1	2	2	1	0	0
AC-130A	11	7	8	8	8	8	12
B-57G	10	10	10	9	9	10	10
F-4D	63	60	55	63	67	81	69
Udorn							
F-4D	36	37	36	32	31	38	36

TABLE A-2

USAF STRIKE RESOURCES IN THE REPUBLIC OF VIETNAM AS OF END OF MONTH

	Apr	May	Jun	Jul	Aug	Sep	Oct
Bien Hoa							
A-37B	27	27	24	25	26	26	26
Da Nang							
A-1H	2	2	2	0	0	0	0
AC-119K	7	6	4	4	3	3	0
F-4D/E	54	54	56	59	56	58	54
Phan Rang							
AC-119G/K	12	13	13	14	6	0	0
F-100D/F	66	65	62	17	0	0	0
Phu Cat							
F-4D	38	39	36	33	35	39	11
Tan Son Nhut							
AC-119G	10	10	10	10	1	0	0

TABLE A-3

TOTAL SORTIES FLOWN AND PORTION FLOWN IN STEEL TIGER BY U.S. STRIKE RESOURCES IN SOUTHEAST ASIA

USAF		May	Jun	Jul	Aug	Sep	Oct	Total
A-1	SEA	323	233	220	324	277	216	1593
Steel Tiger	(SL)	186	88	120	150	100	112	756
A-37	SEA	40	1148	881	610	120	1055	3854
	SL	0	0	0	0	0	0	0
AC-119	SEA	345	503	369	311	138	111	1777
	SL	178	103	43	45	59	49	477
AC-130	SEA	320	277	155	160	184	179	1275
	SL	265	126	83	72	109	103	758
B-52	SEA	1282	1030	1047	1050	1010	1019	6438
	SL	1026	647	680	584	512	596	4045
B-57	SEA	247	163	76	81	5	178	750
	SL	247	163	52	31	2	110	605
F-4	SEA	5991	4984	3284	3633	4289	3734	25915
	SL	3586	2665	1652	1231	1910	2101	13145
F-100	SEA	1884	1221					3105
	SL	1508	509					2017
F-105	SEA	372	235	189	205	209	188	1398
	SL	32	0	2	0	0	0	34
USAF Total	SEA	10804	9794	6221	6374	6232	6680	46105
	SL		4301	2632	2113	2692	3071	21837

TABLE A-3

TOTAL SORTIES FLOWN AND PORTION FLOWN IN STEEL TIGER BY U.S. STRIKE RESOURCES IN SOUTHEAST ASIA
(Continued)

		May	Jun	Jul	Aug	Sep	Oct	Total
Navy								
A-4	SEA	106						106
	SL	100						100
A-6	SEA	536	427	345	333	72	207	1920
	SL	535	421	344	321	72	197	1890
A-7	SEA	1803	1966	1603	1503	1075	740	8690
	SL	1706	1565	1223	1210	1035	720	7459
F-4	SEA	385	325	239	282	67	204	1502
	SL	355	305	162	221	67	204	1314
Navy Total	SEA	2830	2718	2187	2118	1214	1151	12218
	SL	2696	2291	1729	1752	1174	1121	10763
US Total	SEA	13634	12512	8408	8492	7446	7831	58323
	SL	9724	6592	4361	3865	3866	4192	32600

TABLE A-4

OBSERVED TARGET DAMAGE IN STEEL TIGER

Type Target	15-31 May	Jun	Jul	Aug	Sep	Oct	Total
Trucks							
Destroyed	504	252	86	30	68	46	986
Damaged	490	299	175	69	141	51	1225
Fires	657	161	59	21	28	23	949
Sec Exp	425	284	86	70	102	62	1029
TKP/STO							
Tac Air							
Fires	678	57	29	90	204	134	1192
Sec Exp	381	224	138	540	1497	781	3561
Defenses							
Guns Des	62	34	31	9	18	19	173
Guns Dam	8	9	8	17	12	4	58
Fires	137	7	0	1	2	0	147
Sec Exp	76	11	3	10	3	1	104
LOCs							
Tac Air							
Cuts	786	768	637	530	232	328	3281
Slides	66	57	92	93	38	36	382
Arc Light							
Sec Exp	174	95	29	28	28	147	501
OTHER							
Fires	569	228	154	102	134	243	1430
Sec Exp	309	308	140	89	177	173	1196

TABLE A-5

U.S. STEEL TIGER SORTIES EXPENDING ORDNANCE
BY TARGET TYPE STRUCK ON FIRST STRIKE

	15-31 May	Jun	Jul	Aug	Sep	Oct	Total
Lines of Communication	1532	2033	1591	1000	487	667	7310
Truck Parks and Storage Areas	608	1143	791	1054	984	952	5532
Trucks	976	782	263	163	270	210	2664
Defenses	387	192	54	57	110	121	921
Other	754	940	312	414	1220	730	4370
Total	4257	5090	3011	2688	3071	2680	20797

TABLE A-6

STEEL TIGER SORTIES EXPENDING ORDNANCE
BY TARGET TYPE STRUCK ON FIRST STRIKE - F-4

	15-31 May	Jun	Jul	Aug	Sep	Oct	Total
LOCs	481	861	629	241	287	364	2863
Storage	270	629	384	415	543	487	2728
Trucks	482	355	131	105	155	133	1361
Defenses	347	147	50	46	80	115	785
Other	340	387	143	182	547	401	2000
Total	1920	2379	1337	989	1612	1500	9737

TABLE A-7

STEEL TIGER SORTIES EXPENDING ORDNANCE
BY TARGET TYPE STRUCK ON FIRST STRIKE - F-100

	15-31 May	Jun	Jul	Aug	Sep	Oct	Total
LOCs	664	298					962
Storage	83	81					164
Trucks	26	24	(F-100s were returned to				50
Defenses	27	17	the U.S. in June)				44
Other	152	89					241
Total	952	509					1461

TABLE A-8

STEEL TIGER SORTIES EXPENDING ORDNANCE BY TARGET TYPE STRUCK ON FIRST STRIKE - AC-119K

	15-31 May	Jun	Jul	Aug	Sep	Oct	Total
Trucks	49	38	12	3	9	4	115
Other	32	42	15	27	27	35	178
Total	81	80	27	30	36	39	293

TABLE A-9

STEEL TIGER SORTIES EXPENDING ORDNANCE BY TARGET TYPE STRUCK ON FIRST STRIKE - AC-130

	15-31 May	Jun	Jul	Aug	Sep	Oct	Total
Storage	3	3	2	2	17	31	58
Trucks	99	57	40	22	32	23	273
Other	9	6	1	18	23	24	81
Total	111	66	43	42	72	78	412

TABLE A-10

STEEL TIGER SORTIES EXPENDING ORDNANCE BY TARGET TYPE STRUCK ON FIRST STRIKE - B-57

	15-31 May	Jun	Jul	Aug	Sep	Oct	Total
LOCs	9	29	3	1	0	2	44
Storage	17	32	23	14	2	47	135
Trucks	53	33	12	11	0	14	123
Other	31	53	0	2	0	15	101
Total	110	147	38	28	2	78	403

TABLE A-11

STEEL TIGER SORTIES EXPENDING ORDNANCE BY TARGET TYPE STRUCK ON FIRST STRIKE - A-1

	15-31 May	Jun	Jul	Aug	Sep	Oct	Total
Storage	23	30	14	26	8	16	117
Trucks	2	0	4	6	0	1	13
Defenses	1	0	4	2	8	4	19
Other	74	38	54	62	58	76	362
Total	100	68	76	96	74	97	511

TABLE A-12

STEEL TIGER SORTIES EXPENDING ORDNANCE BY
TARGET TYPE STRUCK ON FIRST STRIKE - A-6

	15-31 May	Jun	Jul	Aug	Sep	Oct	Total
LOCs	124	159	178	148	11	55	675
Storage	55	39	110	108	33	81	426
Trucks	34	23	9	4	1	3	74
Defenses	4	10	0	1	2	0	17
Other	33	45	23	31	18	39	189
Total	250	276	320	292	65	178	1381

TABLE A-13

STEEL TIGER SORTIES EXPENDING ORDNANCE BY
TARGET TYPE STRUCK ON FIRST STRIKE - A-7

	15-31 May	Jun	Jul	Aug	Sep	Oct	Total
LOCs	254	686	781	610	189	246	2766
Storage	157	329	258	489	381	290	1904
Trucks	231	252	55	12	73	32	655
Defenses	8	18	0	8	20	2	56
Other	83	280	76	92	547	140	1218
Total	733	1565	1170	1211	1210	710	6599

TABLE A-14

BARREL ROLL SORTIES EXPENDING ORDNANCE BY
TARGET TYPE STRUCK ON FIRST STRIKE - F-4

	15-31 May	Jun	Jul	Aug	Sep	Oct	Total
LOCs	32	60	46	50	18	47	253
Storage	337	486	266	292	370	304	2055
Trucks	23	92	45	28	42	38	268
Defenses	39	145	66	24	48	62	384
Other	256	306	161	262	350	254	1589
Total	687	1089	584	656	828	705	4549

TABLE A-15

BARREL ROLL SORTIES EXPENDING ORDNANCE BY
TARGET TYPE STRUCK ON FIRST STRIKE - AC-119K

	15-31 May	Jun	Jul	Aug	Sep	Oct	Total
Trucks	9	10	9	1	9	25	63
Other	43	100	50	42	39	36	310
Total	52	110	59	43	48	61	373

TABLE A-16

BARREL ROLL SORTIES EXPENDING ORDNANCE BY TARGET TYPE STRUCK ON FIRST STRIKE - AC-130

	15-31 May	Jun	Jul	Aug	Sep	Oct	Total
Trucks	0	0	0	1	17	12	30
Other	4	23	7	44	35	4	117
Total	4	23	7	45	52	16	147

TABLE A-17

BARREL ROLL SORTIES EXPENDING ORDNANCE BY TARGET TYPE STRUCK ON FIRST STRIKE - A-1

	15-31 May	Jun	Jul	Aug	Sep	Oct	Total
Storage	19	20	4	8	14	14	79
Defenses	12	20	8	2	8	2	52
Other	31	89	64	64	112	62	422
Total	62	129	76	74	134	78	553

TABLE A-18

UNIT STRIKE AIRCRAFT SORTIE RATES
(Sorties per Possessed Aircraft)

Unit Aircraft	May	Jun	Jul	Aug	Sep	Oct
8TFW						
B-57G	0.8	0.6	0.4	0.4	0.4	0.6
AC-130	1.0	0.9	0.7	0.8	0.9	0.5
F-4	1.0	0.8	0.6	0.6	0.7	0.3
12TFW						
F-4	0.8	0.8	0.5	0.7	0.8	1.3
56SOW						
A-1	0.5	0.4	0.3	0.4	0.6	0.5
AC-119K	---	---	---	---	---	0.4
315TAW						
A-37B	---	---	---	1.1	1.1	1.5
366TFW						
F-4	1.0	0.9	0.6	0.6	1.2	1.1
388TFW						
F-105	0.8	0.6	0.6	0.6	0.7	0.6
F-4	1.0	0.9	0.6	0.8	0.8	0.7
432TRW						
F-4	0.9	0.8	0.5	0.5	0.7	0.6
14SOW (Inactivated Sep)						
AC-119G	0.6	0.6	0.4	0.6	---	---
AC-119K	0.6	0.7	0.5	0.5	---	---
35TFW (Inactivated Jul)						
A-37	1.6	1.6	1.4			
F-100	1.0	0.7	0.1			

TABLE A-19

FIXED-WING USAF AIRCRAFT

HIT AND LOSS EXPERIENCE

Steel Tiger	Sorties Flown	Sorties Reporting AAA Reactions	Aircraft Hit	Aircraft Lost
15-31 May	3115	588	2	0
Jun	7039	444	7	3
Jul	3985	106	5	2
Aug	4098	99	7	0
Sep	4508	125	11	1
Oct	4424	83	3	1
Total	27169	1445	35	7
Barrel Roll				
15-31 May	705	15	0	0
Jun	1637	37	4	1
Jul	1766	38	2	1
Aug	1030	52	6	1
Sep	1420	64	9	4
Oct	1078	67	0	0
Total	7636	273	21	7

TABLE A-20

USAF FAC RESOURCES
BY BASE AS OF END OF MONTH

	Apr	May	Jun	Jul	Aug	Sep	Oct
Bien Hoa							
O-1E	2	0	0	0	0	0	0
O-2A	64	61	52	42	0	0	0
O-2B	7	5	0	0	0	0	0
OV-10A	25	25	23	23	0	0	0
Cam Ranh Bay							
O-2A	44	44	41	40	29	0	0
Da Nang							
O-2A	54	53	46	56	49	49	42
O-2B	6	5	5	5	5	0	0
OV-10A	33	32	44	44	45	46	32
Korat							
OV-10A	6	5	3	4	7	6	0
Nakhon Phanom							
O-2A	14	14	12	2	12	12	0
OV-10A	27	28	14	14	13	12	18
Phan Rang							
O-2A	0	0	0	0	36	71	89
O-2B	10	13	18	13	13	13	9
OV-10A	0	0	0	0	21	20	25

TABLE A-21

USAF RECONNAISSANCE RESOURCES
BY BASE AS OF END OF MONTH

	Apr	May	Jun	Jul	Aug	Sep	Oct
Cam Ranh Bay							
RC-130B	6	5	4	5	0	0	0
Da Nang							
EC-47Q	10	11	12	11	10	11	5
Korat							
EB-66C/E	23	22	15	15	15	15	14
EC-121D/T	5	4	3	0	0	0	0
EC-121R	8	9	9	9	9	6	6
Nakhon Phanom							
QU-22B	17	17	17	17	14	20	14
EC-47N/P/Q	6	6	5	5	5	5	0
Phu Cat							
EC-47N/P	17	16	17	17	19	20	18
Tan Son Nhut							
EC-47N/P	17	18	19	19	17	16	16
RB-57E	3	3	3	3	0	0	0
RF-4C	19	17	19	17	0	0	0
Udorn							
RF-4C	21	23	20	21	22	21	20

TABLE A-22

FAC SORTIES BY COUNTRY AIRCRAFT TYPE

	May	Jun	Jul	Aug	Sep	Oct	Total
Steel Tiger							
O-2	767	523	373	354	465	507	2989
OV-10	1075	655	562	652	671	755	4370
F-4	189	227	231	244	223	214	1328
UC123	41	---	---	---	---	---	41
Total	2072	1405	1166	1250	1359	1476	8728
Barrel Roll							
O-2	5	---	---	---	2	5	12
OV-10	47	79	32	33	37	65	293
F-4	69	77	93	101	83	66	489
UC123	56	28	---	---	---	---	84
Total	177	184	125	134	122	136	878
RVN							
O-2	969	985	1003	1107	1043	691	5798
OV-10	576	520	538	683	705	433	3455
Total	1545	1505	1541	1790	1748	1124	9253
Cambodia							
A-1	1	---	---	---	---	---	1
O-2	973	672	502	513	512	401	3573
OV-10	513	540	349	438	521	212	2573
F-4	---	---	2	5	---	---	7
Total	1487	1212	853	956	1033	613	6154
SEA Total	5281	4306	3685	4144	4262	3349	25027

APPENDIX B
ENEMY RESOURCES
Personnel

Table B-1 shows the number of enemy estimated to be in Laos on the 15th of each month. Not included are an estimated 14,000 to 15,000 Communist Chinese, of whom it is estimated 3,000 to 3,500 served on AAA crews, and the rest on road construction teams and in other support organizations. The intelligence information about the Communist Chinese was of a much more tenuous nature than that about the North Vietnam Army.[1]

Lines of Communication
Input Corridors

From North Vietnam the enemy used four major input routes to bring supplies into Laos: Mu Gia and Ban Karai Passes, Ban Raving, and the complex of roads through the western end of the DMZ, which are shown in Figure B-1 on the next page. The Laotian route structure began to fan out as it left the North Vietnam-Laos border, providing the enemy with many alternate routes. NVN Route 15 led into Mu Gia Pass, where it became Route 12 with alternates 1201 and 1202, leading into the Route 23 complex of the central route structure. NVN Route 137 was the input route to Ban Karai Pass, where it became Route 912 and led to the Route 91 complex. NVN Route 1039 was the Ban Raving entry route, and NVN Routes 1032 and 1036 crossed into Laos at the DMZ. All connected with Laos Route 92, which led to the Route 91 complex, but Route 1032 also continued into Laos until it met Route 9.

In addition, the enemy made some use of the pipeline system described in the Commando Hunt V report.[2]

Central Route Structure

The principal north-south corridors of the central route structure were the Route 23, 91, 92, and 96 complexes. Each had proliferated as the enemy reacted to the results of LOC interdiction over the past several years.

Exit Corridors

The principal exit corridors into the RVN were along Routes 922 and 925; the principal throughput route into Cambodia was 110. The east end of the latter, Route 110E, led through the tri-border area into RVN. Each of these exit routes had alternates and by-passes.

Road Proliferation

After 26 February 1971, the cutoff date stated in the Commando Hunt V report, the construction of another 220 kilometers of new roads was photo-confirmed by 7AF Intelligence. The bulk of this construction took place prior to the start of Commando Hunt VI.[3]

Input and Throughput

Calculations based on sensor-detected truck movements and visual observation of trucks by aircrews and road-watch teams provided estimates of tonnages of supplies input into Steel Tiger, and throughput into the

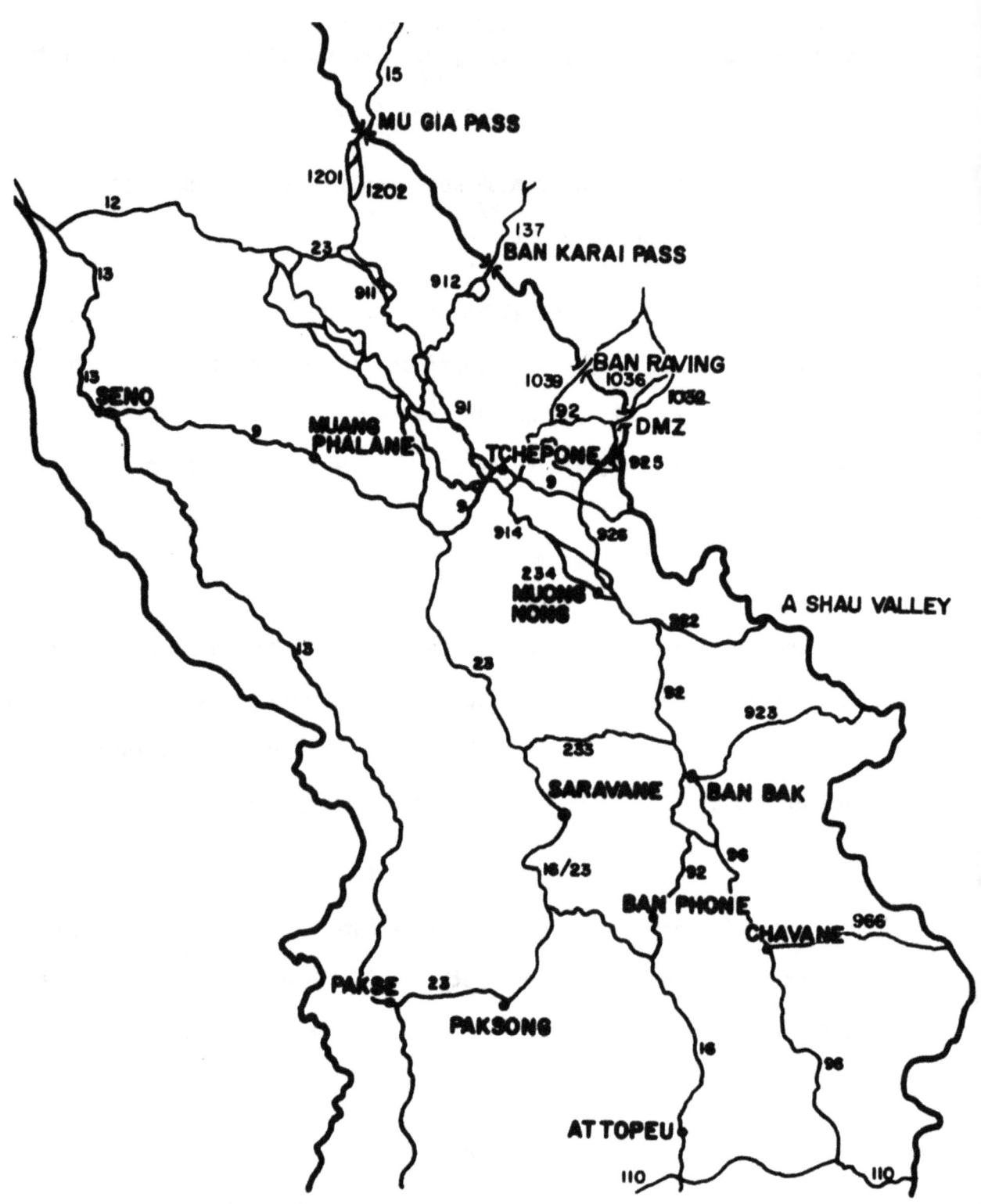

STEEL TIGER ROUTE STRUCTURE

Figure B-1

RVN or Cambodia. TFA analyzed sensor-detected truck movements to eliminate duplicate movements by the same truck through more than one sensor string. After eliminating sensor duplicates, a comparison of these truck movements with visual truck observations eliminated more duplicate counts. Then the number of trucks visually observed but not detected by sensors was added to the sensor-detected truck movements to arrive at total truck movements on a route. Those numbers were multiplied by three, three and a half, or four tons per truck, depending on the latest intelligence estimate, to provide tonnage estimates.[4]

Input

Truck movements into Steel Tiger from NVN provided estimates of input tonnages. In addition, supplies entered Laos through the pipeline. Based on the number of truck movements, stockpile buildup, and target damage assessment, an estimated average POL input of 1.5 tons per day entered through the pipeline during the course of the campaign. There was no estimated input via Waterway 7, which had made a minor contribution toward the input total during Commando Hunt V. Table B-2 shows the estimated input into Laos during Commando Hunt VI.[5]

Throughput

Subtraction of southbound trucks destroyed between the final sensor string of the exit routes and the Laotian border from the southbound sensor-detected truck movements recorded by these strings provided an estimate of trucks entering the RVN and Cambodia. Multiplying this figure by the current intelligence estimate of tons per truck gave an estimate of throughput tonnage. Table B-3 shows the estimated throughput into the RVN and Cambodia during Commando Hunt VI.[6]

Enemy Defenses

AAA

The number of active guns in Steel Tiger decreased for the first half of the campaign, and held steady for the second half (Table B-4). Seventh Air Force Intelligence derived these estimates from all sources, but primarily from observed firings. It was believed that many guns were placed in storage during the campaign, rather than returned to NVN.[7]

SAMs

During Commando Hunt VI, the enemy maintained approximately 200 SAM sites in NVN, of which he kept about 15 percent operational. The four sites he is known to have established in Laos during Commando Hunt V never became operational during Commando Hunt VI.[8]

MIGs*

During Commando Hunt VI, significant North Vietnam Air Force (NVNAF) activities included construction on several NVN airfields, MIG presence south of 20 degrees north, and two MIG incursions into Laos. Four hangarettes were built at Quang Lang, the runway at Dong Hoi was extended to 7,500 feet, and the runways at Na San and Dien Bien Phu were improved.[9] (See Figure B-2, for map of NVN airfields.)

---

*Soviet jet fighter aircraft, named after the designers, Mikoyan and Gureyevich.

The MIGs which were at Bai Thuong at the start of the campaign had redeployed to the north by the end of May, but MIGs returned south on 20 August. For the rest of the campaign, NVAF maintained a MIG presence south of 20 degrees north, primarily at Bai Thuong, except during and immediately after Typhoon Hester in late October. This was the first time the NVAF had occupied a southern NVN airfield for an extended period during the rainy season. In past years, the wet-season pattern had been not to deploy south of 20 degrees north at all until late in October. [10/]

On 4 October a MIG, apparently staging from Dong Hoi, attempted to intercept an Arc Light cell in the Tchepone area. This was the first known NVAF attempt to attack a B-52, and the farthest known southern incursion of MIG aircraft. On 13 October, a MIG penetrated Laotian airspace in northeast Barrel Roll. [11/]

Also, in September and October, some 30 MIGs that had been located in southern China for several years were returned to NVN. [12/] This may be taken as an indication that the enemy considered his northern airfields to be as safe from Allied attack as those in China.

TABLE B-1

ENEMY ORDER OF BATTLE IN LAOS

	NVA	Laotian	Total
May	63055	40480	103535
Jun	59030	39350	98380
Jul	59980	39050	99030
Aug	56290	39465	95755
Sep	58090	39290	97380
Oct	56590	39115	95705

TABLE B-2

INPUT IN TONS, BY ROUTE

Route	15-31 May	Jun	Jul	Aug	Sep	Oct	Total
Mu Gia	670	425	101	0	78	256	1530
Ban Karai	540	555	52	48	70	120	1385
Ban Raving	543	197	66	3	10	13	832
DMZ	445	210	61	12	15	3	746
Pipeline	121	79	24	10	13	13	260
Total	2319	1466	304	73	186	405	4753

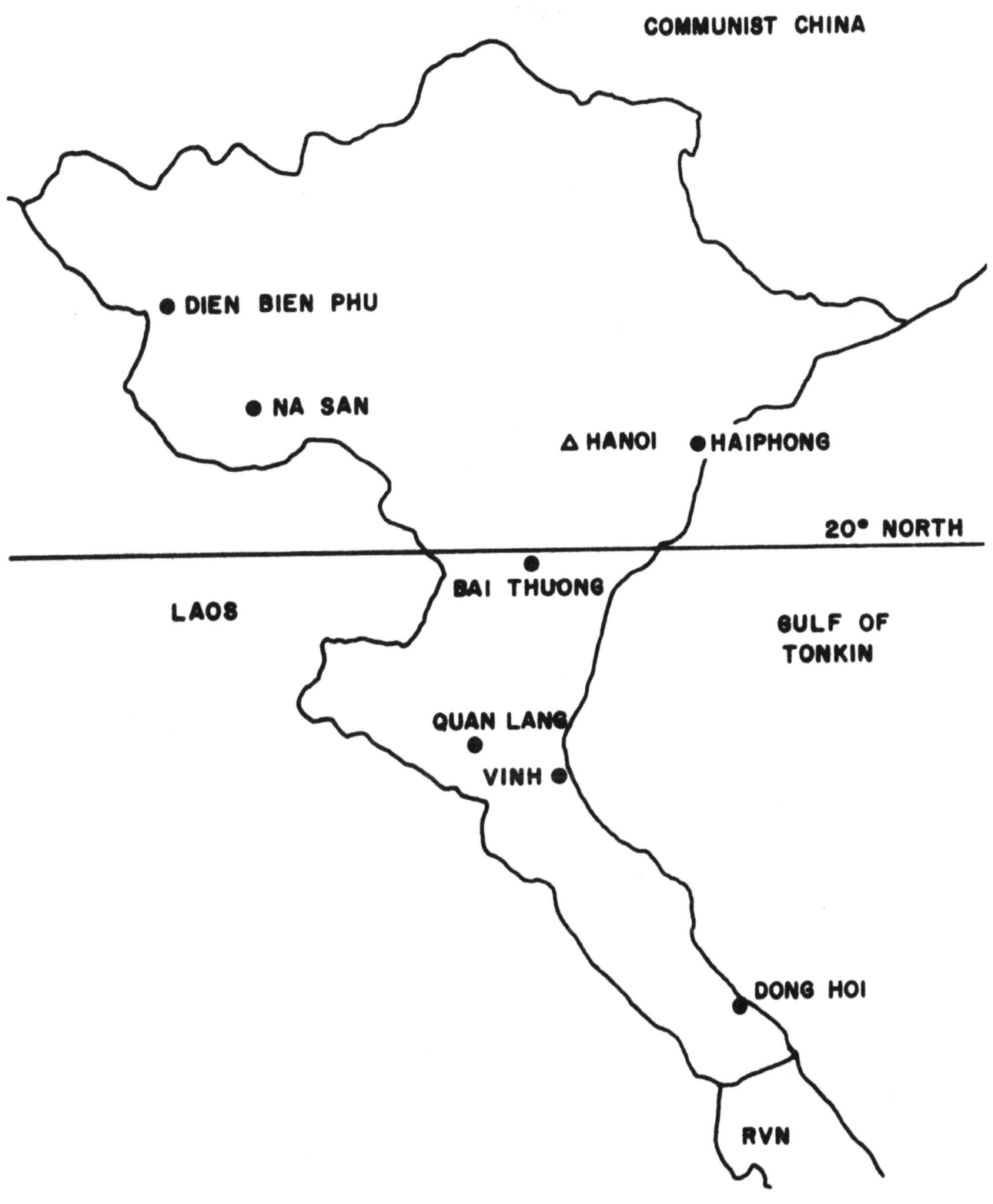

NORTH VIETNAM AIRFIELDS

Figure B-2

TABLE B-3

THROUGHPUT IN TONS, BY ROUTE

Route	15-31 May	Jun	Jul	Aug	Sep	Oct	Total
925	177	134	6	3	21	0	341
9H	33	49	0	0	0	0	82
926	65	27	3	0	0	0	95
921B	0	7	0	0	0	0	7
922	240	96	14	36	0	0	386
966C/D	36	24	27	42	0	9	138
110D/E	42	65	11	0	0	0	118
110A	176	23	19	21	0	0	239
Total	769	425	80	102	21	9	1406

TABLE B-4

AAA ORDER OF BATTLE
AVERAGE BY MONTH

BARREL ROLL

Weapon Type	15-31 May	Jun	Jul	Aug	Sep	Oct	Average
23mm	27	17	6	1	0*	3	7
37mm	41	31	19	12	8	13	19
57mm	0	0	0	0*	1	2	1
Total	68	48	25	13	9	18	27

STEEL TIGER

Weapon Type	15-31 May	Jun	Jul	Aug	Sep	Oct	Average
23mm	151	140	110	92	94	93	102
37mm	412	343	280	263	259	254	299
57mm	59	48	24	14	13	20	29
100mm	6	6	0	0	2	0	2
Total	628	537	414	369	368	367	432

*Average greater than zero but less than .5.

APPENDIX C

CAMPAIGN RESULTS IN OTHER AREAS

Republic of Vietnam

Ground Operations

Enemy-initiated activity in the RVN (Table C-1) was less in the wet season than in the preceding dry season. An anticipated enemy "celebration" on 19 May, Ho Chi Minh's birthday, did not materialize. This was attributed to continued supply shortages and deployment difficulties. Allied insertions in the LAM SON 720 area of operation (AO) kept pressure on the enemy's logistic system in the A Shau Valley.[1/] (See Figure C-1, for map of RVN.)

On the night of 23 May, a sapper attack on Cam Ranh Bay destroyed six POL tanks, causing the loss of 1,680,000 gallons of JP-4 and 210,000 gallons of aviation gas. There were 213 attacks by fire (ABFs) during the week of 19 through 26 May, the highest weekly total of the season. The next week provided the season highs for ground assaults, incidents of terrorism, and resultant friendly casualties (killed/wounded/abducted) with 39, 288, and 672, respectively.

In May, enemy contact with allied forces took place primarily in the LAM SON 720 AO and in the B-3 Front, especially in Kontum Province. In June, ABFs in MR-1 increased after allied maneuvers in the LAM SON 720 AO were terminated. Da Nang Air Base (AB) received ABFs on 5 and 7 June; however, enemy activity in general was directed against Vietnamese installations.[3/]

From 20 through 22 June, Fire Support Base (FSB) Fuller in northern MR-1 came under an AFB and a ground attack, which failed. On 23 June, two more ground attacks were repulsed, but the ABFs continued and, that evening, ARVN elements destroyed their own artillery and withdrew. Friendly artillery and tac air were directed on the base as enemy troops reportedly occupied it. 4/

Sappers struck in Qui Nhon Harbor in Binh Dinh Province on several occasions. On 14 June an explosion damaged the U.S. merchant ship American Hawk, which was grounded against a pier. Three empty ammunition barges were sunk on 25 July, as was the merchant ship SS Green Bay on 17 August. Two Korean ammunition barges were sunk in Qui Nhon Harbor on the evening of 23 September. On the 26th a Vietnamese explosive ordnance disposal team removed a mine containing 180 pounds of TNT from the hull of the Panamanian freighter Lucky II. In nearby Qui Nhon City, from 23 through 30 June, ABFs and suspected sabotage resulted in the destruction of over 6,000 tons of ammunition and most of the ARVN storage point facilities. 5/

Elsewhere the most notable act of sabotage occurred on 25 August, when sappers detonated four ammunition revetments around the perimeter of the Cam Ranh Bay ammunition storage area. Results were 6,000 tons of ammunition, with an estimated value of 8 to 10 million dollars, destroyed; $96,000 damage to other USAF real estate, including a badly damaged radar site (only minor damage to electronic equipment inside); and one wounded. 6/

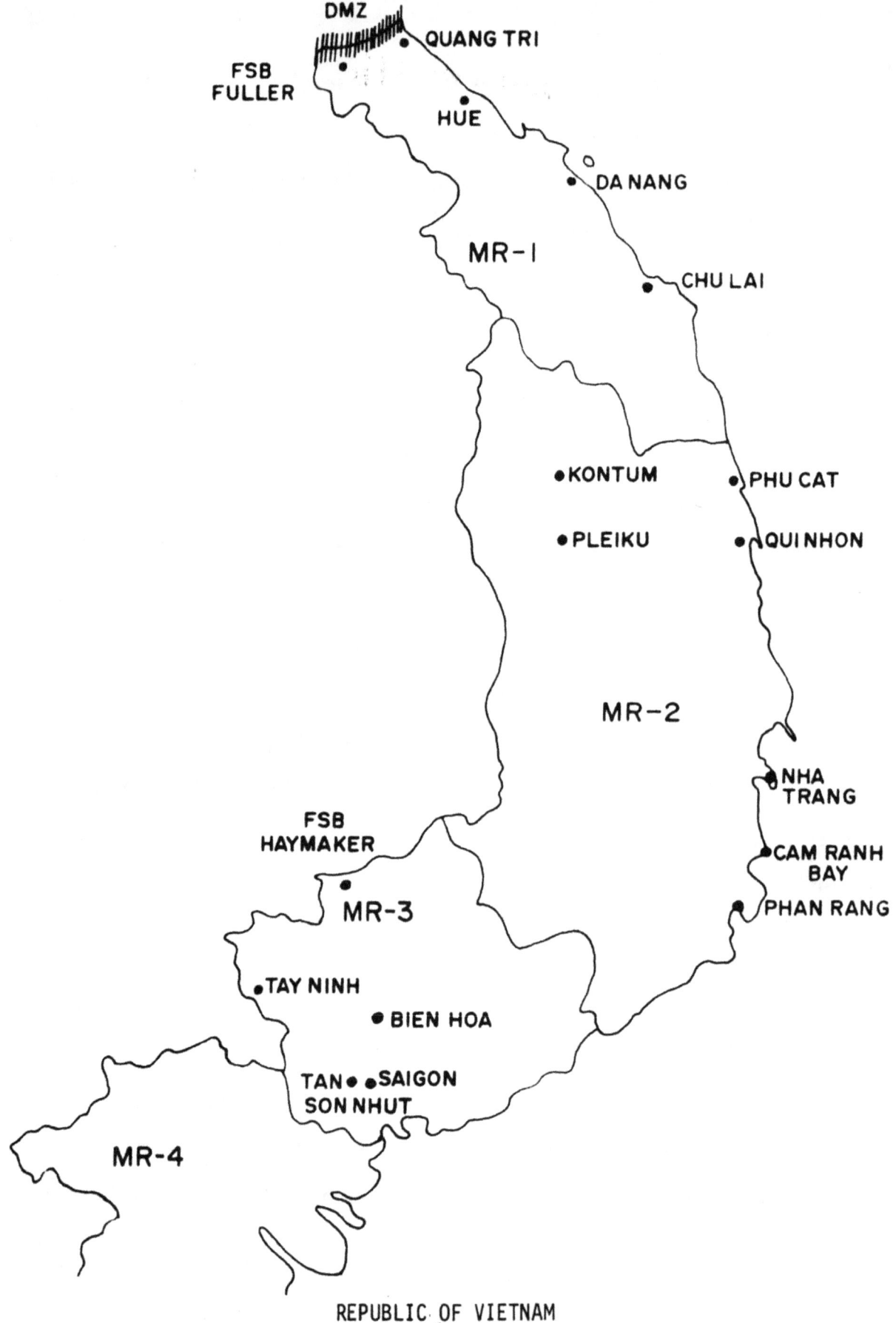

REPUBLIC OF VIETNAM

Figure C-1

Enemy-initiated activity increased in August but did not disrupt South Vietnamese congressional elections which were held on the 29th. This pattern was repeated for the 3 October presidential elections, in which President Thieu was overwhelmingly reelected. ABFs on Da Nang AB and Bien Hoa AB on 3 October did not cause any casualties. 7/

Operation LAM SON 810 began on 6 September in western Quang Tri Province, under the control of the 1st ARVN Division, and ended on 20 September. The objectives were to destroy enemy supplies and bases and to interdict enemy LOCs. United States forces were to occupy rear defensive positions to free ARVN forces for combat operations. 8/

On 13 September, RVN forces found 15,000 gallons of oil and other enemy supplies. This was the most notable event of the operation. Enemy losses were 125 killed, one detained, and 32 individual and 11 crew-served weapons captured. Friendly losses were 15 killed and 70 wounded. 9/

As the wet season ended, enemy activity in MR-1 decreased, possibly as a result of flooding in southern NVN. The only significant activity was in the outlying districts of Saigon, as the enemy attempted a show of force prior to the 31 October Presidential Inauguration. There were 38 firebombings in the city during October, many of them against U.S. vehicles. However, the Inauguration proceeded on schedule. 10/

Air Operations

Throughout the campaign, the VNAF was expected to, and did, assume an increased responsibility for the conduct of the air war in the RVN.

In every month the majority of the attack sorties in the RVN was flown by the VNAF (Table C-2), which flew two-thirds of such sorties for the entire campaign. United States resources were used only as required. Increased enemy activity in August resulted in more USAF attack sorties than any other month.[11/]

The successes of ARVN forces boosted the Vietnamization program and increased its chances of success. The VNAF flew 32 percent of the attack sorties in SEA (Table C-3), averaging 117 per day, compared with 108 per day during Commando Hunt V. Reported bomb damage from US (Arc Light excluded) and RVN air forces is shown in Table C-4.[12/]

Results of Arc Light strikes in the RVN are shown in Table C-5. Throughout the campaign, 43 percent of the sorties reported RNO.[13/]

Cambodia

The enemy strategy in Cambodia was believed to be one of protracted warfare, employing probing attacks, attacks by fire, and occasional ground attacks against selected targets. During the wet season, he could be expected to attack small urban areas around Phnom Penh and cities located on key roads and waterways. In eastern Cambodia, he would attempt to expand, consolidate, and protect his logistic system and LOCs, meanwhile developing sources of foodstuffs, other supplies, and manpower. In the west, he would try to obtain control over the rich rice-growing areas and thus force the FANK to extend themselves and increase their vulnerability to attack.[14/]

The USAF mission in Cambodia was to maintain surveillance of enemy activities and to attack and interdict them to protect US forces in the RVN. This mission included support of FANK troops, since their activity could cause the enemy to expend supplies that otherwise might have been moved into the RVN.[15]

Ground Operations

Just before Commando Hunt VI began, the FANK had opened Pich Nil Pass for the first time in a month, and convoys had begun to reach Phnom Penh from the port of Kompong Som.[16] (See Figure C-2 for map of Cambodia.)

The only activity in Cambodia as the wet season started was the ARVN operation in MR-1. On 15 May, an ARVN ranger battalion discovered and appropriated a 100-ton rice cache. United States Air Force tac air and gunships and ARVN troops repulsed an enemy attack on a supply convoy, which proceeded to Phnom Penh without further incident. On 26 and 27 May, ARVN units near Snuol engaged enemy forces in heavy combat. On 28 May, the ARVN began moving toward the RVN border and were attacked several times before reaching FSB Haymaker on 31 May. United States Air Force tac air destroyed much of the equipment and supplies that were left behind as the ARVN departed. Official ARVN results of the operation from 26 to 31 May were 1143 enemy killed. Friendlies lost 37 killed, 167 wounded and 74 missing.[17]

An enemy campaign, presumably an attempt to secure the Tonle Toch River near Phnom Penh as an LOC, opened in late May as two FANK battalions in that area were nearly overrun. United States gunships supported the friendlies and were credited with at least 50 killed by air (KBA). Meanwhile USAF C-130s and VNAF C-119s flew numerous resupply sorties. Two C-130s sustained heavy damaged from groundfire.[18] (See Figure C-3 for map of Tonle Toch AO.)

On 8 June a FANK relief column was ambushed a mile east of Vihear Suor, coming under a heavy mortar attack. The column fell back to Vihear Suor. After further reinforcements had been received, FANK units resumed their offensive on 18 June. By 23 June, they had reached their objective at Kompong Chamlang. FANK units reported that supporting USAF air strikes had caused numerous enemy casualties. VNAF airlifted supplies and equipment to the FANK units.[19]

Following this victory, a three-pronged FANK operation, involving 39 battalions, commenced. Its objective was to secure and hold the major outposts and towns between the Tonle Toch River and the Mekong River. After successfully meeting their objective, the FANK ended the operation on 20 July. The entire Tonle Toch operation was officially terminated on 6 August.[20]

Total casualties reported by the US Defense Attache's Office in Phnom Penh and by MACV were 193 friendlies killed, 1,238 wounded, and 858 enemy killed. FANK figures showed 1,356 enemy killed. Twenty-six VNAF sorties and 1,051 USAF sorties expended. The Khmer Air Force (KAF) flew more than 400 sorties. The only aircraft lost was a KAF UH-1H helicopter. USAF-reported BDA included 252 bunkers and 12 sampans

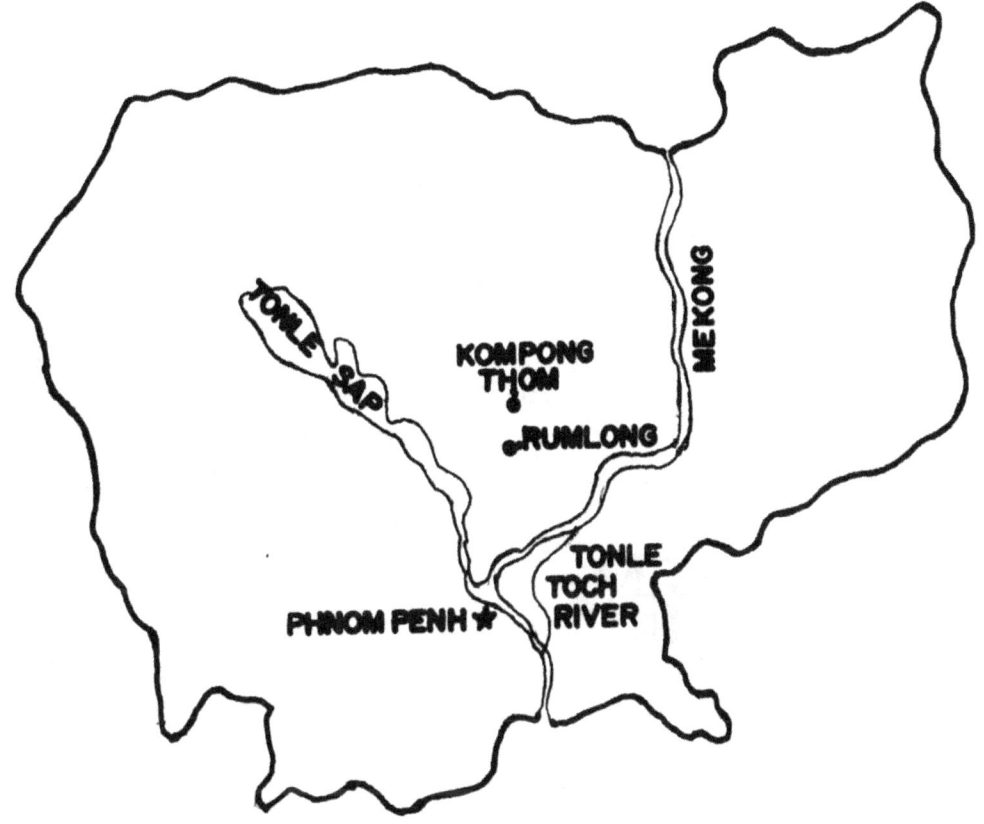

CAMBODIA

Figure C-2

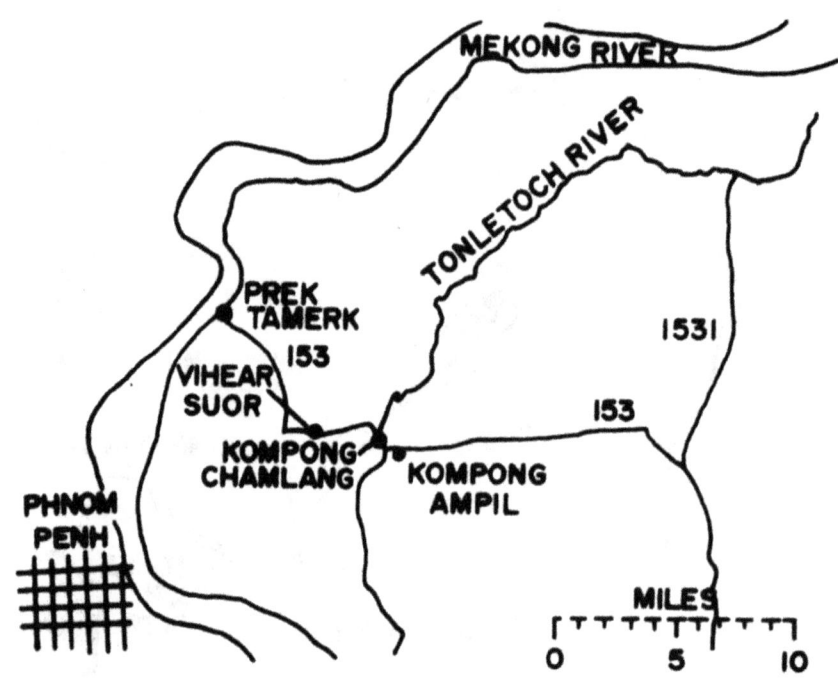

TONLETOCH AREA OPERATIONS

Figure C-3

destroyed or damaged, 13 TICs broken, 625 KBA, and 313 secondary explosions and fires.[21]

For the first time in the war, FANK forces had defeated an enemy main-force unit. With this success, the Cambodians began to take the war to the enemy.[22]

The next major FANK operation was Operation CHENLA II, an attempt to clear Route 6 to Kompong Thom, which was friendly-held but surrounded. (See Figure C-4 for map of CHENLA II AO.) On 24 August, 10 FANK battalions supported by USAF tac air and gunships and Cambodian tanks, took Rumlong. By the evening of 31 August, they had taken Kompong Thma. Large enemy supply caches were found in sweeps around Kompong Thma. United States Air Force airstrikes supported the sweeps which, by 15 September, were estimated to have freed 12,000 villagers from enemy control.[23]

Elsewhere in Cambodia, on the morning of 20 September, an enemy rocket attack damaged or destroyed 14 of 29 storage tanks in the POL storage area just north of Phnom Penh. Since the tanks were only partially filled, the loss was not critical.[24]

FANK forces began pushing northward from Kompong Thma toward Kompong Thom, and on 24 September a 24-ship convoy began moving from Kompong Chhnang via the Stung Sen River toward Kompong Thom. The convoy came under heavy attack but, after numerous delays, arrived safely in Kompong Thom on 29 September with much-needed supplies. On 6 October, FANK troops from Kompong Tham linked up with those from Kompong Thom. The breakthrough was a significant link for government forces, even though the route was not secure enough for truck convoys because the enemy held nearby Santuc Mountain.[25]

FANK attention rapidly shifted to that enemy stronghold, USAF tac air supported the attack. Friendly forces occupied the top of the mountain on 14 October.[26]

On 23 October, the enemy was able to bring Pich Nil Pass under recoilless rifle fire and effectively close it for the remainder of the month. The KAF, aided by USAF FACs, supported FANK counterattacks.[27]

The enemy remained in the CHENLA II area, and was able to resume the offensive on 26 October, after destroying a vital bridge on Route 6 23 miles north of Phnom Penh, which aggravated the critical supply situation for friendly forces. By 29 October, virtually all friendly forces in the CHENLA II area were under attack. Forces in Rumlong were cut off both north and south. As the month ended, enemy pressure seemed to center on Rumlong.[28]

Enemy attacks against ARVN increased as the RVN Presidential election neared. However, the enemy achieved no notable success from these attacks.[29]

Air Operations

The USAF employed the concept of QRF sorties to conserve resources. United States Air Force aircraft were thus able to strike lucrative targets, if available, and provide air support, if needed, without flying

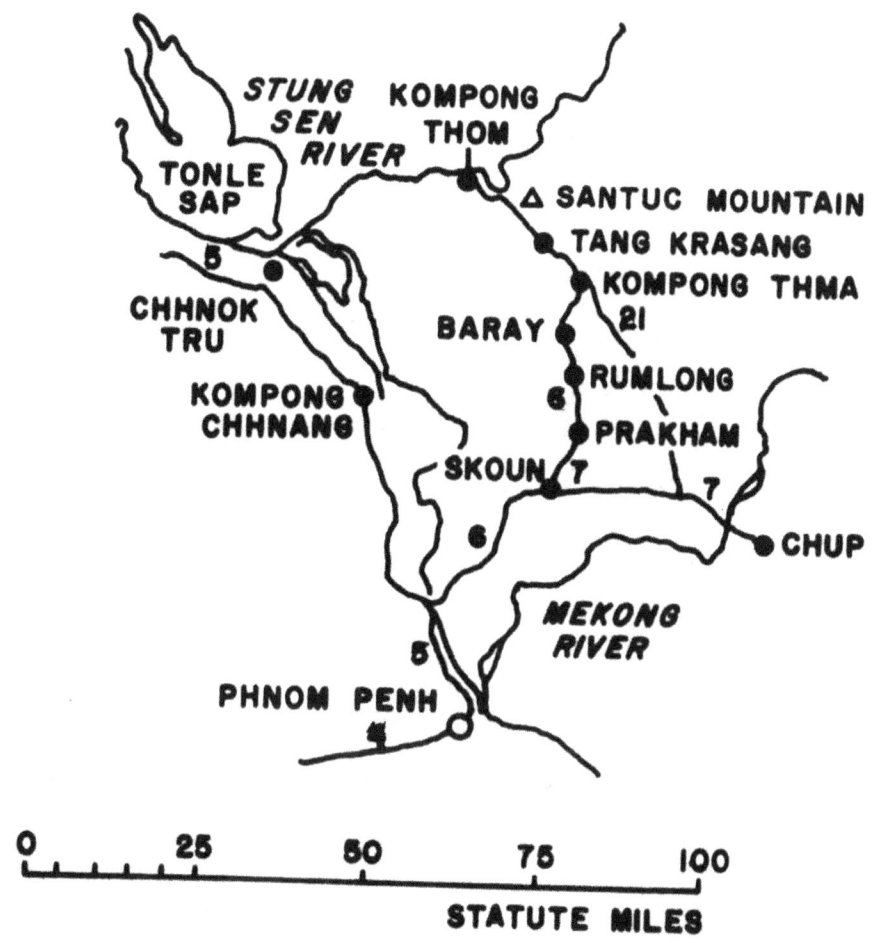

CHENLA II AREA OF OPERATIONS

Figure C-4

sorties when such targets were not available. Table C-6 shows the number of sorties flown by USAF and VNAF aircraft. United States Air Force aircraft averaged 21 preplanned and 13 QRF sorties per day, compared with 18 and 22, respectively, during Commando Hunt V. [30/]

Table C-7 shows reported results from Allied air sorties during Commando Hunt VI. Table C-8 shows the results of Arc Light strikes. Over the season, 54 percent of the Arc Light sorties reported RNO. [31/]

Barrel Roll

As Commando Hunt VI opened, the enemy offensive against Luang Prabang had been stopped, as was his advance southward toward Vientiane. [32/] (See Figure C-5 for map of Barrel Roll.)

It was expected that the enemy would continue to maintain sufficient military forces in Barrel Roll to insure ground superiority over friendly forces at chosen points, and that he would launch small-unit to battalion-size attacks against friendly bases south and west of the PDJ in an effort to keep friendly forces off balance and prevent them from posing a serious threat to his positions in that area. The enemy was expected to react sharply to any Allied incursions toward his supply complexes in the Ban Ban area. It was anticipated that neither side would be able to advance farther during the wet season that they had during the previous dry season. [33/]

TAC AIR activities were to be devoted to close air support of pro-government forces and strikes against truck parks, storate areas, and

IDPs. Special systems were to be used against enemy truck activity.[34/]

Ground Operations

As Commando Hunt VI started, pro-government units were conducting offensives north and northeast of Luang Prabang, meeting only occasional resistance. It appeared that the efforts of Allied air and government artillery had effectively stopped the enemy offensive in the Luang Prabang area. Meanwhile, government irregulars were starting to advance on the PDJ from their positions at Sam Thomg and Long Tieng.[35/] (See Figure C-6 for map of PDJ.)

Enemy activity consisted primarily of attacks on several Lima Sites* (LS) northeast of the PDJ, which friendly forces had held and were using as staging areas for attacks against enemy LOCs. A ground assault against LS-32 was repulsed on 14 June, with support from AC-130 and AC-119K gunships. On 29 June, LS-06 fell to a 200- to 300-man attack.[36/]

The irregulars reached the southern edge of the PDJ in early June, and continued to advance. In mid-July, enemy resistance stiffened and an increased use of PT-76 tanks in the central PDJ was noted. United States Air Force tac air struck several enemy high-ground positions north of LS-22, eliminating stubborn resistance.[37/]

*Temporary aircraft landing sites in Laos.

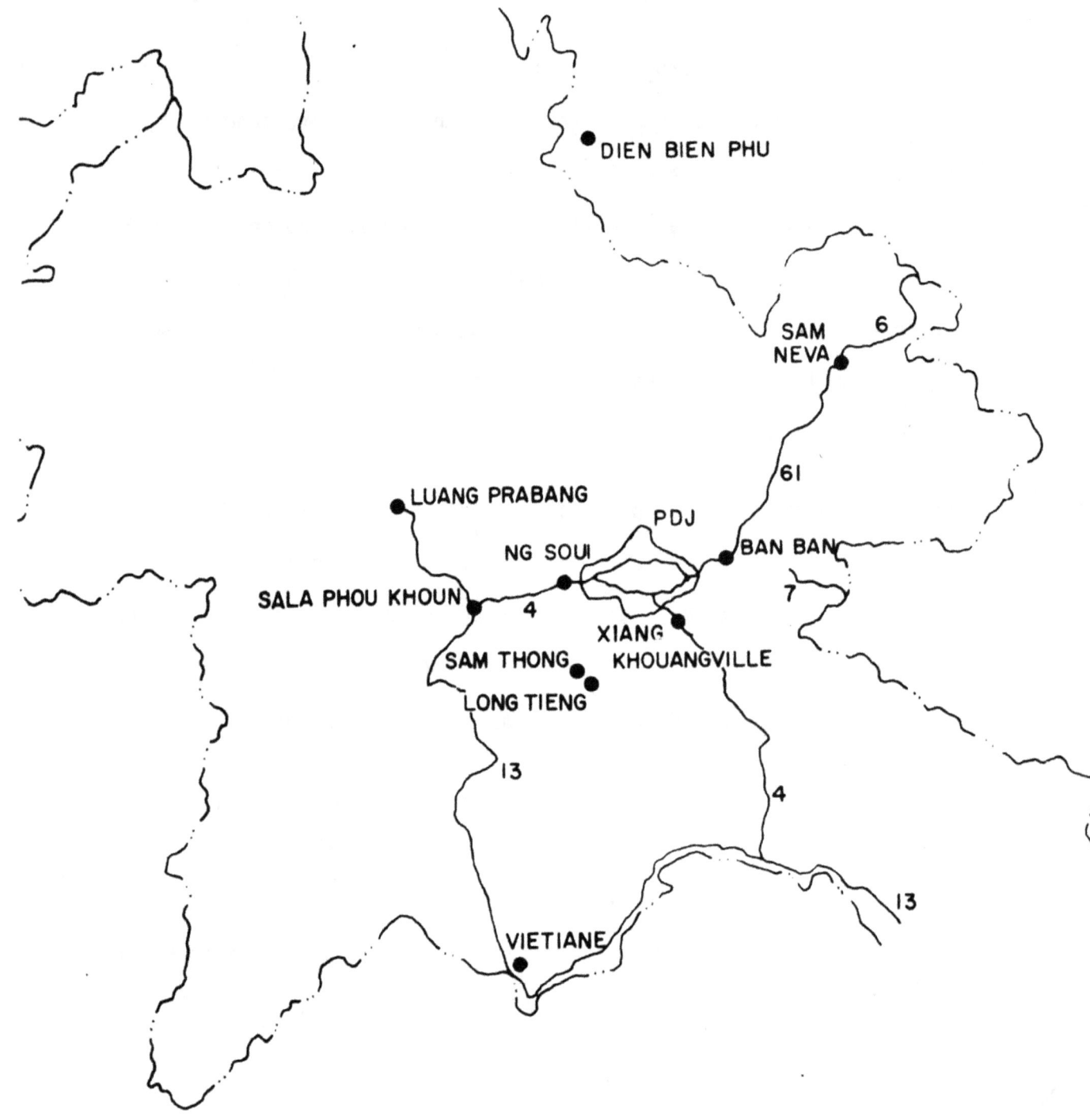

BARREL ROLL

Figure C-5

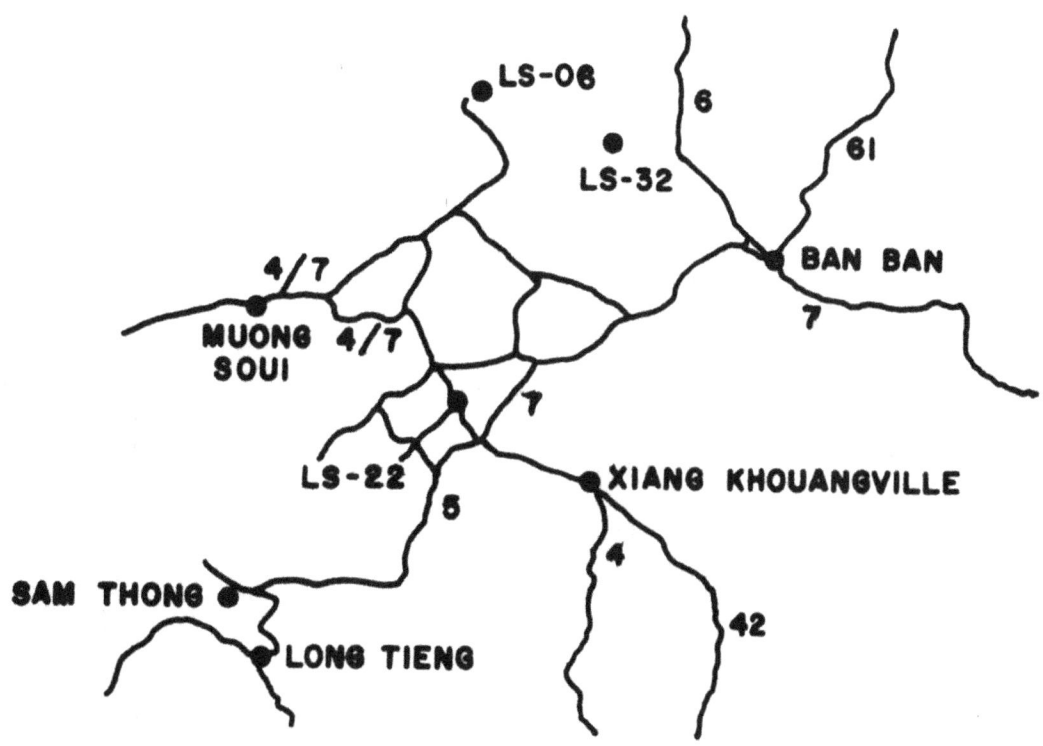

PLAIN OF JARS AREA

Figure C-6

Patrols from friendly forces were reported to be within 1,000 meters of Xiang Khouangville. Seizure of that town would have placed pro-government forces in control of Routes 4 and 72, both suspected enemy supply routes into the PDJ. However, the enemy brought reinforcements into the PDJ area and, in early August, drove friendly forces back from Xiang Khouangville, which they held for the rest of the campaign. 38/

On 5 August, pro-government forces initiated Operation Golden Mountain from Sala Phou Khoun to retake Muong Soui. Irregular forces, with Royal Laotian Air Force (RLAF) gunship support, advanced east along Route 4 against heavy resistance. In mid-August, the advance was stopped 34 kilometers west of its goal, as air support was limited by adverse weather. However, in mid-September, an airborne assault on an enemy-held airstrip brought the RLG forces to within 22 kilometers of Muong Soui. On 24 September, they took the Muong Soui airstrip. The town was occupied the next day, although enemy harassment of the occupying force continued through October. 39/

Ground activity on the PDJ was at a low level in late October, as both sides prepared for the dry season. Adverse weather restricted the use of air support. 40/

Air Operations

The USAF flew an average of 34 sorties daily in Barrel Roll, compared to 36 during Commando Hunt V. Overall, over one-eighth of the US sorties flown in SEA were flown in Barrel Roll, about three percent higher than the planning figure. The RLAF averaged over 2900 direct air support and air interdiction sorties monthly, by far the majority of attack sorties flown in Barrel Roll. However, the RLAF T-28s delivered much lighter bomb loads than the USAF F-4s and A-1s, and RLAF AC-47 gunships had significantly less firepower than the USAF AC-119Ks.[41/]

In late July, tac air began striking IDPs on Route 7, and succeeded in closing two of them the first week. In early August, a vulnerable highway segment was struck repeatedly for four days, resulting in numerous cuts and slides and the closing of the IDP for six weeks. It was closed once again, for one day, in early October.[42/]

Table C-9 shows the distribution of US effort. Table C-10 shows the emphasis (43 percent) placed on close air support in employing US tactical air strikes, and Table C-11 gives the BDA reported.

TABLE C-1

NUMBER OF ENEMY-INITIATED ACTIONS IN RVN

	ABFs	Ground Assaults	Incidents	Terrorism Killed/Wounded/Abducted
Jan	537	52	714	1373
Feb	638	100	786	1542
Mar	871	137	877	2177
Apr	770	132	1031	2773
May	533	111	1034	1288
Jun	525	105	840	1517
Jul	190	57	635	998
Aug	347	61	643	1041
Sep	328	78	624	869
Oct	437	28	713	974
Jan-May Total	3349	532	4442	9153
Jun-Oct Total	1827	329	3455	5399
Monthly Average	518	86	790	1455

TABLE C-2

US AND VNAF ATTACK SORTIES IN RVN

	USAF			NAVY	VNAF			TOTAL
	Preplanned	QRF	Gunship		Preplanned	QRF	Gunship	
15-31 May	465	253	22	89	1481	21	19	2350
Jun	880	428	48	415	2293	9	21	4094
Jul	745	189	17	453	2775	13	30	4222
Aug	1237	167	47	379	3227	0	34	5091
Sep	701	458	17	36	3387	20	33	4652
Oct	351	603	11	30	2665	0	50	3710
TOTAL	4379	2098	162	1402	15828	63	187	24119

TABLE C-3

US AND VNAF ATTACK SORTIES IN SEA

	USAF			NAVY	VNAF			TOTAL
	Preplanned	QRF	Gunship		Preplanned	QRF	Gunship	
RVN	4379	2098	162	1402	15828	63	187	24119
Barrel Roll	4620	372	650	--	--	--	--	5642
Cambodia	3518	2279	749	--	3716	47	89	10398
Steel Tiger	10056	1642	1064	8407	--	--	--	21169
	22573	6391	2625	9809	19544	110	276	61328

TABLE C-4

ALLIED BDA SUMMARY IN RVN

	Secondaries		Structures		Bunkers		
	Fires	Explosions	Des	Dam	Des	Dam	KBA
15-31 May	102	162	322	66	1158	324	218
Jun	172	397	650	101	1855	577	113
Jul	229	384	766	204	2024	605	136
Aug	213	587	783	166	2094	608	91
Sep	133	296	790	161	2239	674	61
Oct	86	167	312	153	1197	577	77
Total	935	1993	3623	851	10567	3365	696

TABLE C-5

ARC LIGHT RESULTS IN RVN

	Sorties	Secondary Explosions	Explosions per Sortie	RNO Sorties
15-31 May	37	15	.41	19
Jun	274	118	.43	152
Jul	325	234	.72	127
Aug	379	129	.34	175
Sep	338	156	.46	113
Oct	145	33	.23	56
Total	1498	685	.46	642

TABLE C-6

USAF AND VNAF ATTACK SORTIES IN CAMBODIA

	USAF			VNAF			
	Preplanned	QRF	Gunships	Preplanned	QRF	Gunship	Total
15-31 May	425	259	101	680	0	13	1478
Jun	1178	459	219	849	20	12	2737
Jul	574	299	207	783	18	3	1884
Aug	493	281	124	473	9	5	1385
Sep	423	470	57	221	0	18	1189
Oct	425	511	41	710	0	38	1725
Total	3518	2279	749	3716	47	89	10398

TABLE C-7

RESULTS OF ALLIED TAC AIR STRIKES IN CAMBODIA

	Secondaries		Trucks	
	Fires	Explosions	Destroyed	Damaged
15-31 May	175	182	0	2
Jun	427	146	25	13
Jul	884	171	11	22
Aug	226	150	1	5
Sep	208	216	2	6
Oct	128	130	4	13
	1448	995	43	61

TABLE C-8

ARC LIGHT RESULTS IN CAMBODIA

	Sorties	Secondary Explosions	Explosions Per Sortie	RNO Sorties
15-31 May	67	68	1.01	37
Jun	63	18	.29	46
Jul	42	2	.05	23
Aug	52	9	.17	28
Sep	143	22	.13	84
Oct	229	98	.43	104
Total	596	217	.36	322

TABLE C-9

USAF ATTACK SORTIES IN BARREL ROLL

Attack Sorties	15-31 May	Jun	Jul	Aug	Sep	Oct	Total
Preplanned	536	1158	657	657	886	726	4620
QRF	64	63	6	92	72	75	372
Gunship	71	157	93	88	141	100	650
Total	671	1378	756	837	1099	901	5642

TABLE C-10

US ATTACK SORTIES IN BARREL ROLL BY TARGET TYPE

	15-31 May	Jun	Jul	Aug	Sep	Oct	Total
Fighter-Attack:							
LOCs	32	60	46	50	18	47	253
Truck Parks/ Storage Areas	356	506	270	300	384	318	2134
Trucks	23	92	45	28	42	38	268
Defenses	51	165	74	26	56	64	436
Close Air Support	287	395	225	326	462	316	2011
Gunships:							
Trucks	9	10	9	2	26	37	93
Close Air Support	47	123	57	86	74	40	427
Total	805	1351	726	818	1062	860	5622

TABLE C-11

TOTAL US BDA IN BARREL ROLL

BDA	15-31 May	Jun	Jul	Aug	Sep	Oct	Total
Fires	50	136	73	83	200	124	666
Explosions	182	419	220	268	398	197	1684
Struct Des	39	66	58	117	100	139	519
Struct Dam	25	47	34	79	64	36	285
Trucks Des	27	24	10	8	18	12	99
Trucks Dam	29	30	19	4	42	35	159
KBA	109	208	215	114	66	47	759

APPENDIX D
MUNITIONS

During the Commando Hunt VI campaign, US airpower was faced with a wide variety of targets that included trucks, bulldozers, cave and bunker storage areas, AAA weapons, watercraft, and personnel. This diversity of target types required the use of many different types of munitions. The types of munitions are described in the Commando Hunt V Report; however, three items of ordnance were introduced to SEA since the report was published. They are described below.

CBU-52A/B

The CBU-52A/B was an anti-materiel munition designed to destroy trucks and other light materiel targets by fragmentation. The weapon consisted of an SUU-30B/B dispenser, 217 BLU-61A/B bomblets weighing 2.16 pounds each, and a dispenser fuze. The munition was introduced into SEA in May 1971 to determine its operational capability. Only the FMU-56B/B fuze was used in this evaluation, although the weapon could be employed with the FMU-26. The 432nd Tactical Reconnaissance Wing started the initial combat evaluation (ICE) on 5 May 1971 and suspended testing on 21 July 1971 due to poor weather and lack of appropriate targets. The evaluation was scheduled to resume in November 1971.[1/]

The SUU-30B/B was a two-piece canister which was released from the delivery aircraft. The FMU-56B/B radar proximity fuze functioned at a preselected height and opened the two halves of the canister. The BLU-61A bombs then fell into the airstream. The shape of BLU-61A/B was such that it would spin due to aerodynamic flutes, thus arming the internal fuze. The lift generated by randomly oriented spinning bombs produced dispersion. The bomb fuzes functioned on impact, exploding the cyclotol main charge. A tin-zirconium liner provided a short-duration incendiary effect when the 364 30-grain steel fragments were propelled at an average velocity of 5300 feet per second.[2/]

The CBU-52A/B was designed to be compatible with A-1, A-37, F-4 (used in the evaluation), F-100, and F-105 aircraft. It could be delivered from a dive or level flight, and could be released individually or in the ripple mode.[3/]

LUU-2/B

The LUU-2/B was a parachute flare, designed to replace the MK-24 flare, with a much longer burn time. A six-month ICE was started in June 1971, and continued into the Commando Hunt VII period. Flares were tested from A-1, AC-119, AC-130, F-4, O-2, and OV-10 aircraft.[4/]

CBU-55

The CBU-55 was an antipersonnel weapon designed for compatibility with F-4 aircraft. The effect came from the overpressure resulting from the explosion of 80 pounds (per bomblet) of liquid hydrocarbon fuel. The ICE began 25 October 1971.[5/]

APPENDIX E

WEATHER

One of the most important factors in the conduct of war in SEA was the weather. During the southwest monsoon, increasing rainfall in Laos caused roads throughout the Ho Chi Minh trail network to become flooded to the point of impassability. At the same time, lower cloud ceilings and decreased visibility hampered the air interdiction campaign.[1]

Transition to the Southwest Monsoon

With the northward movement of the Intertropical Convergence Zone in late May, air masses moving into SEA come from the southwest instead of from the northeast. The first obstacle encountered by these air masses is the Annam Mountains between Laos and Vietnam. The resultant lifting of the air flow results in widespread cloudiness and precipitation, especially on the western slopes of the mountains.[2]

The eastern coastal areas of the Indochina Peninsula are protected from the above effect by the mountains. The air dries out as it descends the eastward slopes, resulting in a progressive decrease in cloud cover with the onset of the monsoon. Although total cloud amounts for other areas increase during this season, there is actually a decrease along the east coast in the amount of low clouds with bases below 5,000 feet.[3]

Southwest Monsoon Weather Patterns

The frequency of thunderstorms, and resultant low visibility, increases everywhere, especially along the windward slopes of the mountains, during the late afternoon and evening. In some interior areas, thunderstorms occur almost daily.[4/]

By late September, the southwest monsoon weakens rapidly due to the approach of the fall transition. East coastal regions start to be affected by the first surges of the northeast monsoon. Precipitation amounts increase rapidly in this area as they decrease over the rest of Southeast Asia. Tropical storms increase during this time of year and can cause extremely heavy rainfall, high winds, and flooding along the northeast coasts.[5/]

Weather During Commando Hunt VI

During May, the southwest monsoon became established near mid-month as southeast and southerly flow shifted to the southwest, and increased cloudiness and convective activity west of the Annam ridgeline. Typhoon Dinah briefly disrupted the normal wind pattern by passing over Hainan Island on 29 May. Several frontal systems pushed southward during the month and increased cloudiness over SEA, particularly over areas north of the DMZ. The poorest overall weather, especially in Laos, occurred from the 19th until approximately the 24th as weak frontal systems pushed southward. As the month progressed, the increasing southwesterly flow over Laos caused the incidence of variable cloudiness conditions to gradually increase, particularly during the afternoon hours. Rain and thundershowers gradually increased during May. In Cambodia, afternoon clouds with isolated afternoon and evening thundershowers prevailed on most days; however, these conditions posed few problems for air operations.6/

During June, the southwest monsoon prevailed over all of SEA. Extensive low cloudiness prevailed west of the Annam ridgeline with the poorest conditions existing during the early morning hours and some improvement noted on most afternoons. The poorest overall weather during the month occurred from approximately the 14th through the 17th over southern Laos and northern South Vietnam. Two typhoons crossed the South China Sea during the month, causing only a brief interruption in the normal southwest monsoon flow. Cloudiness continued to increase over the RVN with the exception of the east coast. Rain or thundershowers occurred over some parts of Laos on most days. Rainfall was at or above normal in all sections of Steel Tiger. In Cambodia, conditions were generally scattered to occasionally broken even during afternoon hours. Visibility was good except during some afternoon shower activity, which increased over that experienced in May.7/

During July, there was little change from June conditions, as precipitation continued to fall over some sections of SEA on nearly every day of the month. The poorer conditions during the month occurred over the northern portion of the RVN and Laos as Typhoon Harriet (6 July) and Tropical Storm Kim (13 July) moved inland, dissipated, moved across

Northern Laos as tropical storms, and diminished to low-pressure centers
The surges produced later in the month, as Typhoons Jean and Lucy passed
close to the area, also caused poor conditions west of the Annam Ridgeline.[8]

In August, cloud amounts continued to be high, but low ceilings
occurred less frequently than before. Shower and thunderstorm activity
was evident on most days over some parts of the areas. The worst weather conditions were west of the Annam ridgeline during the first 20
days of the month. There was a decrease in low cloudiness throughout
SEA, especially late in the month. In Cambodia, conditions were generally favorable, except for the southwest mountains and eastern Cambodia,
where conditions were generally broken to occasionally scattered.[9]

In September, the worst weather ceilings occurred frequently in
Steel Tiger and the northwestern section of RVN. The coastal area of
SEA and the mountains east of the Annam ridgeline experienced an
increase in low cloudiness, with the worst conditions existing north
of 16° N. The worst overall conditions occurred on the last day of
the month over the northern two-thirds of SEA, as Tropical Storm Della
moved across the NVN panhandle into Laos. There were definite indications that the autumn transition had begun in SEA.[10]

During the first half of October, the flow over SEA shifted from
norheast to southwest. Tropical Storm Elaine made landfall in the
vicinity of Vinh on the 9th. Typhoon Hester entered SEA on the coast

of RVN south of Chu Lai on the 23rd. As Hester moved inland and dissipated, a surge developed in the northeast monsoonal flow and persisted for most of the remainder of the month. Weather conditions east of the Annam ridge deteriorated significantly, resulting in the worst October conditions in SEA. The storms all produced extensive low cloudiness and moderate to heavy precipitation east of the ridgeline, as well as poor conditions throughout Laos. Elsewhere in SEA, conditions did show a slight improvement over September, as shower activity declined in all areas. The onset of the northeast monsoon was the 17th (however, the effects of Typhoon Hester on Steel Tiger were so great that the dry-season campaign was not considered to have started until 1 November).[11/]

Table E-1 shows the number of days each month when the indicated cloud condition prevailed during the morning and afternoon hours. April conditions are included for contrast. The high number of days on which there was cloud cover below 5,000 feet was indicative of the generally bad weather during Commando Hunt VI.[12/]

One effect of weather on air operations is shown in Table E-2, which presents the number of sorties flown versus the number cancelled by weather. Over the six-month period, approximately one-eighth of the USAF, Navy, and VNAF sorties scheduled were cancelled due to weather.[13/]

TABLE E-1

FREQUENCY, IN DAYS, OF PREVAILING CLOUD CONDITIONS IN:

STEEL TIGER - MORNING

	Ceiling Below 5,000 ft	Sctd-Broken Below 5,000 ft	Ceiling Above 5,000 ft	No Ceiling
Apr	0	8	0	22
May	4	14	1	12
Jun	29	0	0	1
Jul	26	3	0	2
Aug	12	8	2	9
Sep	23	7	0	0
Oct	16	10	0	5

STEEL TIGER - AFTERNOON

	Ceiling Below 5,000 ft	Sctd-Broken Below 5,000 ft	Ceiling Above 5,000 ft	No Ceiling
Apr	0	10	0	20
May	4	18	1	8
Jun	23	7	0	0
Jul	18	12	0	1
Aug	12	14	2	3
Sep	15	15	0	0
Oct	15	11	0	5

BARREL ROLL - MORNING

Apr	0	10	1	19
May	8	13	1	9
Jun	16	10	0	4
Jul	24	4	1	2
Aug	20	9	1	1
Sep	13	11	0	6
Oct	13	2	0	16

BARREL ROLL - AFTERNOON

Apr	0	15	0	15
May	3	20	1	7
Jun	9	17	0	4
Jul	15	13	1	2
Aug	13	9	2	7
Sep	6	17	0	7
Oct	14	1	0	16

TABLE E-2

WEATHER CANCELLATIONS,

ATTACK AIRCRAFT BY COUNTRY FRAGGED

	Air Force		Navy		VNAF	
	Flown	Canx	Flown	Canx	Flown	Canx
Laos						
May	7600	139	2505	264	--	--
Jun	5165	456	2058	149	4	0
Jul	2919	724	1527	347	--	--
Aug	2542	364	1546	24	--	--
Sep	3342	131	1234	28	--	--
Oct	3306	580	994	591	--	--
Total	24874	2394	9864	1403	4	0
RVN						
May	1410	167	141	16	2625	443
Jun	1473	64	426	7	2361	875
Jul	1156	227	454	122	2867	597
Aug	1712	199	364	30	3296	669
Sep	1488	148	35	0	3385	717
Oct	1080	103	30	0	2682	1267
Total	8319	908	1450	175	17216	4568

TABLE E-2 (Continued)

WEATHER CANCELLATIONS,

ATTACK AIRCRAFT BY COUNTRY FRAGGED

	Air Force		Navy		VNAF	
	Flown	Canx	Flown	Canx	Flown	Canx
Cambodia						
May	1543	41	--	--	1096	222
Jun	1934	62	8	0	904	159
Jul	1149	54	--	--	837	157
Aug	911	106	--	--	447	2
Sep	946	84	2	0	201	0
Oct	909	22	12	0	705	0
Total	7392	369	22	0	4190	540
Service Total	40585	3671	11336	1578	21410	5108

APPENDIX F

TABLES AND FIGURES

CH VI

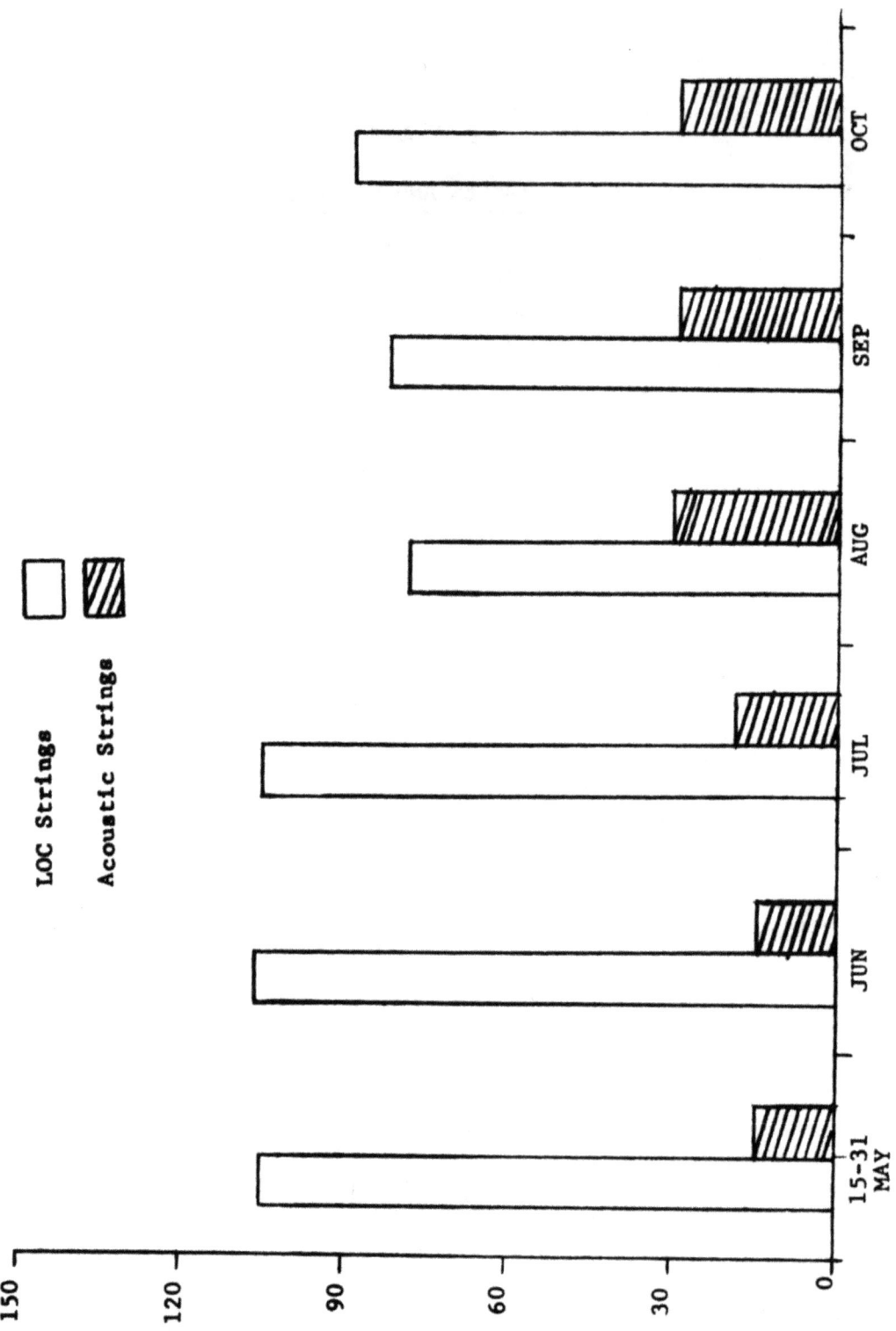

AVERAGE EFFECTIVE SENSOR STRINGS

Figure F-1

TABLE F-1

TRUCKS OBSERVED BY MONTH (OPREP-5)

	15-31 May	Jun	Jul	Aug	Sep	Oct	Total
North							
Day	17	21	13	4	8	10	73
Night	261	72	35	8	11	15	401
South							
Day	39	71	13	15	2	15	155
Night	599	288	94	9	43	111	1144
Parked/Unknown							
Day	360	445	164	159	344	307	1779
Night	760	392	213	67	158	218	1808
Total							
Day	416	537	190	178	354	332	2007
Night	1620	752	342	84	212	344	3354
Total	2036	1289	532	262	566	676	5361

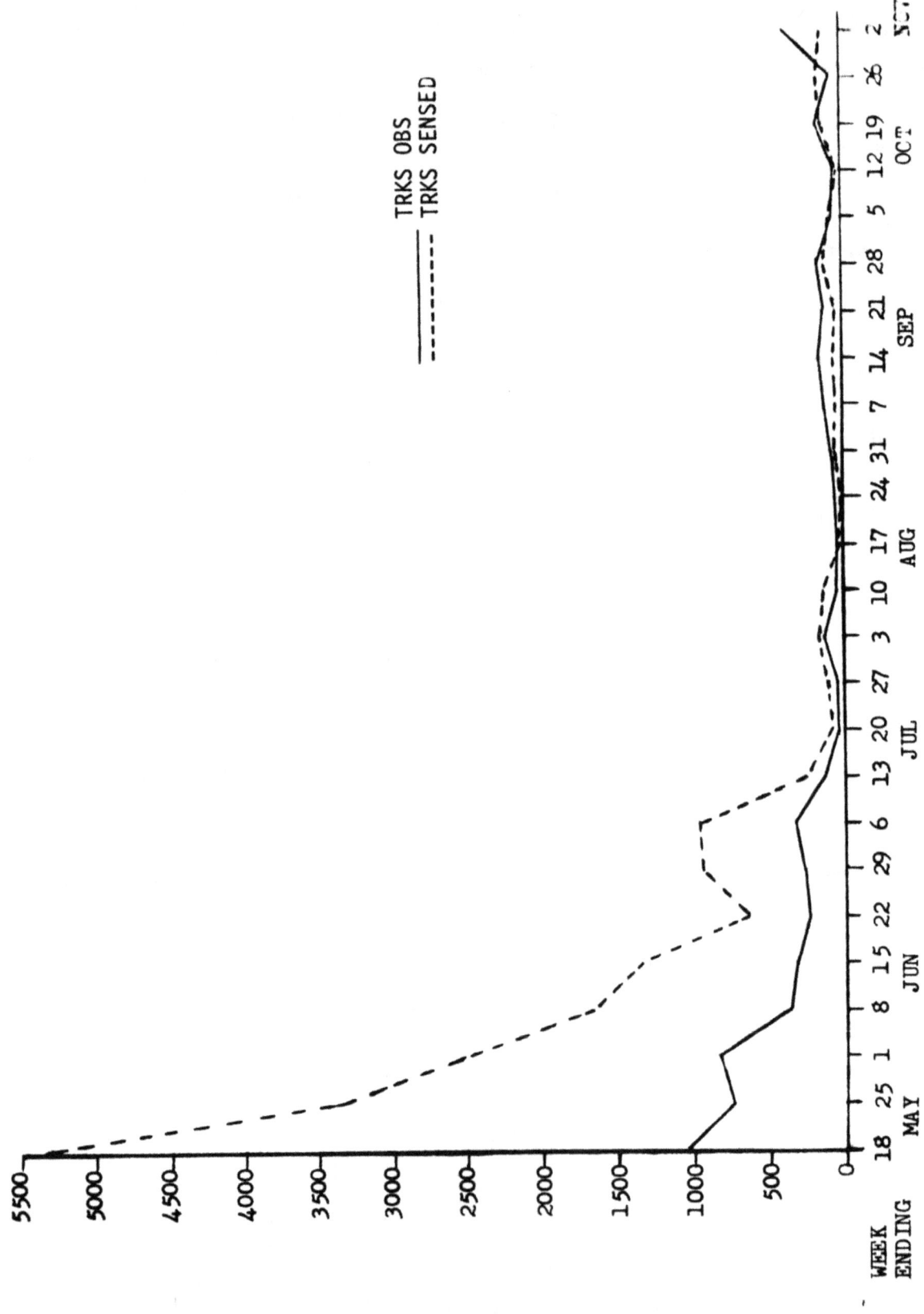

TRUCKS OBSERVED AND SENSOR-DETECTED MOVEMENTS

Figure F-2

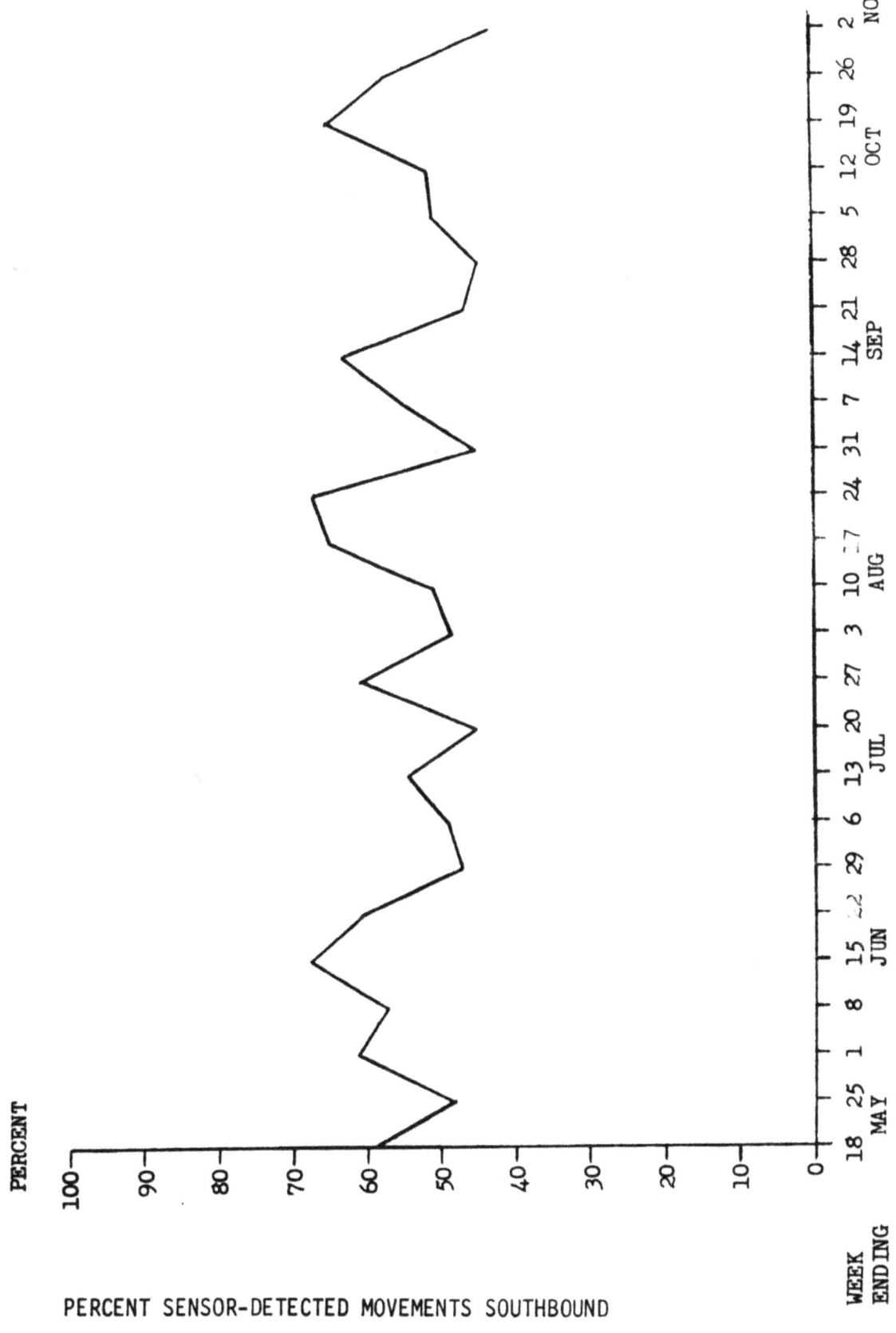

PERCENT SENSOR-DETECTED MOVEMENTS SOUTHBOUND

Figure F-3

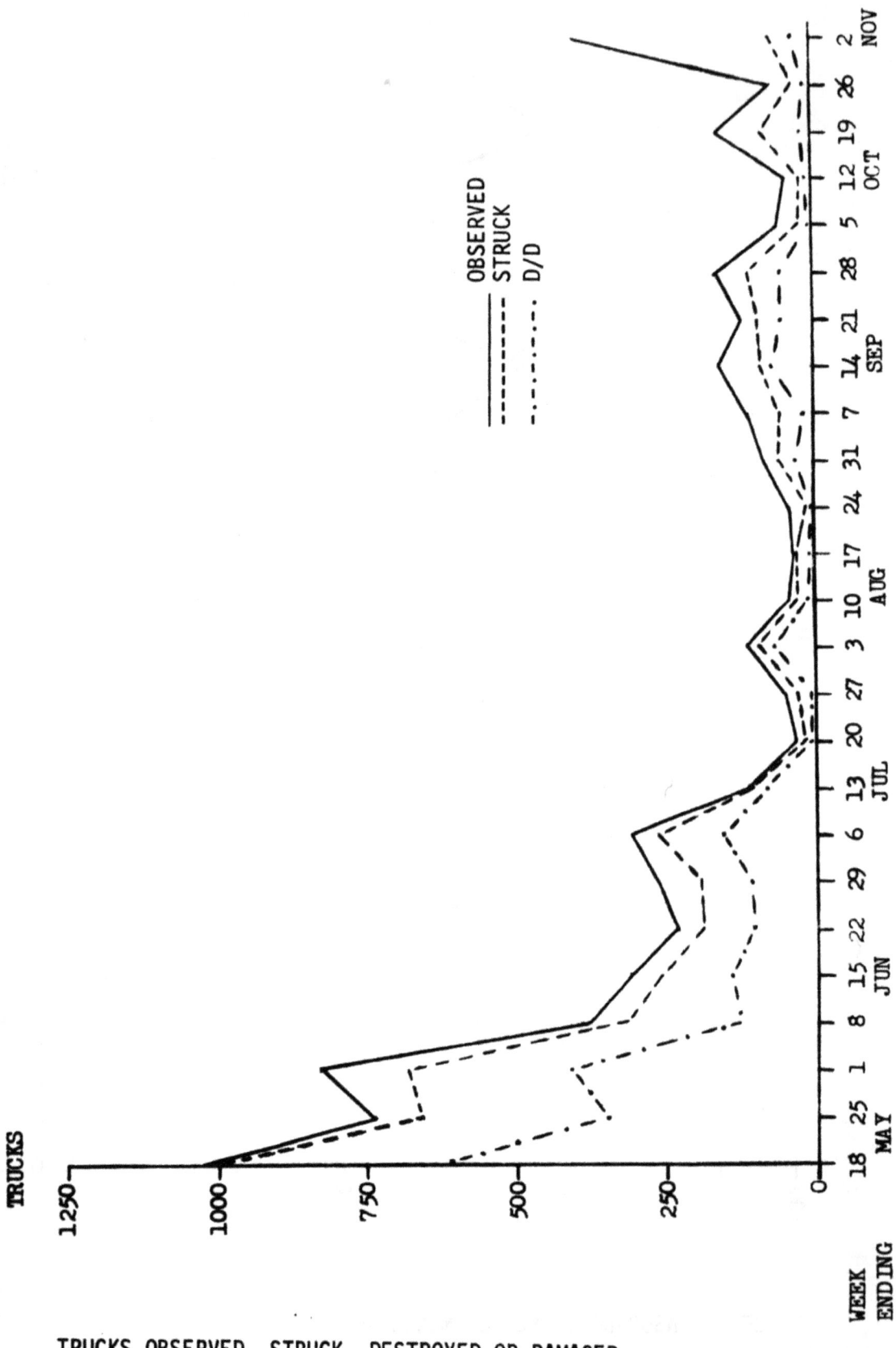

TRUCKS OBSERVED, STRUCK, DESTROYED OR DAMAGED

Figure F-4

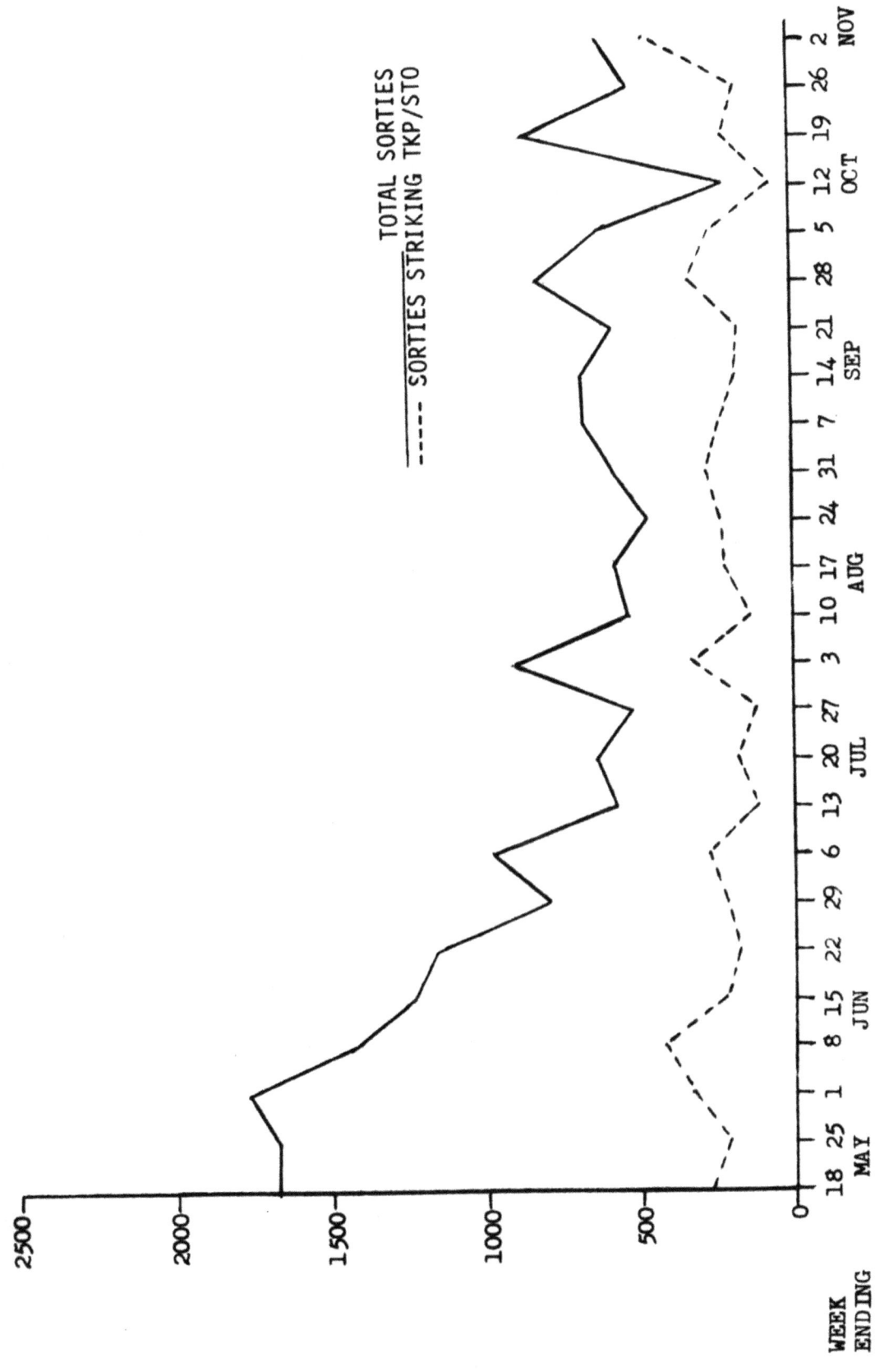

WEIGHT OF EFFORT AGAINST TRUCK PARKS AND STORAGE AREAS

Figure F-5

TABLE F-2
TRUCK PARK AND STORAGE AREA
RESULTS - TACTICAL AIR

	Sorties	Explosions	Fires	Secondaries per Sortie
15-31 May	605	381	678	1.75
Jun	1154	224	57	.24
Jul	793	138	29	.21
Aug	1064	540	90	.60
Sep	986	1497	204	1.73
Oct	937	781	134	.98
Total	5539	3561	1192	.86

TABLE F-3

TRUCK PARK AND STORAGE AREA

RESULTS - ARC LIGHT

	Sorties	Secondary Explosions	Explosions per Sortie	RNO Sorties
15-31 May	290	98	.34	137
Jun	377	114	.30	254
Jul	550	101	.18	356
Aug	532	102	.19	272
Sep	383	84	.22	176
Oct	238	69	.29	123
Total	2370	568	.24	1318

TABLE F-4

COMBAT HIT AND LOSS EXPERIENCE

	15-31 May	Jun	Jul	Aug	Sep	Oct	Total/Avg
Sorties Flown	1967	7039	3985	4098	4508	4424	26021
AAA Reactions	1157	494	104	83	104	80	2022
Aircraft Hit	2	7	5	7	11	3	33
Aircraft Lost	0	3	2	0	1	1	5
Reactions/1000 Sorties	588	70	26	20	23	18	78
Hit/1000 Sorties	1.02	.99	1.25	1.71	2.44	.67	1.27
Lost/1000 Sorties	0	.43	.50	0	.22	.22	.19
Hit/1000 Reactions	1.73	14.17	48.08	84.34	105.77	37.50	16.32
Lost/1000 Reactions	0	6.07	19.23	0	9.62	12.50	2.47

TABLE F-5

SORTIES AND RESULTS AGAINST AAA

	Sorties Flown	Guns Dest	Guns Dam	Guns D/D Per Sortie	Secondary Fires	Secondary Explosions
15-31 May	390	62	8	.18	137	76
Jun	174	34	9	.25	7	11
Jul	56	31	8	.70	0	3
Aug	57	9	17	.46	1	10
Sep	106	18	12	.28	2	3
Oct	121	19	4	.19	0	1
Total	904	173	58	.26	147	104

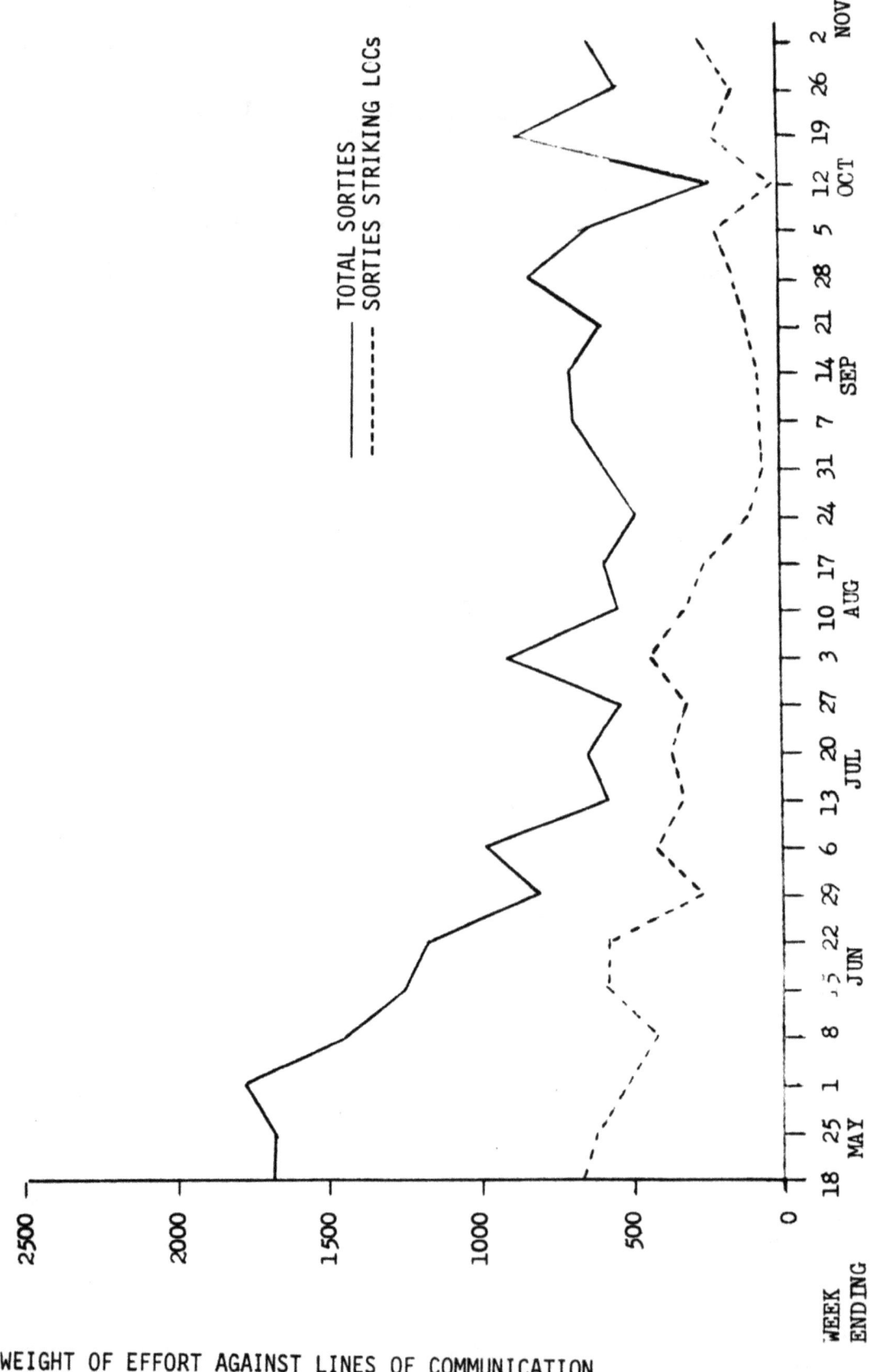

WEIGHT OF EFFORT AGAINST LINES OF COMMUNICATION

Figure F-6

TABLE F-6

SORTIES AND RESULTS AGAINST

LINES OF COMMUNICATION - TACTICAL AIR

	Sorties Flown	Road Cuts	Road Slides	Cuts and Slides Per Sortie
15-31 May	1445	786	66	.59
Jun	2031	768	57	.41
Jul	1591	637	92	.47
Aug	1000	530	93	.62
Sep	488	232	38	.55
Oct	684	328	36	.53
Total	7239	3281	382	.51

TABLE F-7

SORTIES AND RESULTS AGAINST

LINES OF COMMUNICATIONS - ARC LIGHT

	Sorties Flown	Secondary Explosions	Explosions Per Sortie	RNO Sorties
15-31 May	266	174	.65	93
Jun	277	95	.34	177
Jul	97	29	.30	50
Aug	54	28	.52	34
Sep	133	28	.21	67
Oct	338	147	.43	148
Total	1165	501	.43	569

TABLE F-8

TYPICAL SEEDING SEGMENT PACKAGE

Munitions	Sorties	Dispensers	Mines
Gravel (CDU-14)	10	55	79750
WAAPM (CBU-42	2	8	5360
Magnetic Mines (MK-36)	8	N/A	80
Total	20	63	85190

TABLE F-9

ROUTE 103 SEEDING SEGMENTS, SENSOR STRING NUMBERS

Seeding Segment	Initial Seeding	Sensor Number
861	9 Aug 71	33029/33818
862	9 Aug 71	33029/33818
863	9 Aug 71	33789
864	11 Aug 71	33784
865	9 Aug 71	32012/33787
867	25 Aug 71	33121
868	26 Aug 71	33020
871	16 Aug 71	33029/33818

TABLE F-10

MONTHLY EFFORT AGAINST ROUTE 103

	9-31 Aug Sorties	9-31 Aug Weapons	1-30 Sep S	1-30 Sep W	1-31 Oct S	1-31 Oct W	1-10 Nov S	1-10 Nov W	Total S	Total W
WAAPM	44	263	17	82	12	58	7	20	80	423
Gravel	57	308	34	172	28	154	13	83	132	717
MK-36	53	467	8	100	12	116	0	0	73	683
CBU-24	34	278	16	98	17	113	2	12	69	501
CBU-49	37	289	14	93	5	32	0	0	56	414
CBU-52	7	56	3	21	12	88	2	13	24	178
MK-82	6	60	23	256	4	29	0	0	33	345
MK-84 LGB	3	7	1	2	0	0	0	0	4	9
M-118 LGB	1	1	1	1	0	0	0	0	2	2
Total	242	1729	117	825	90	590	24	128	473	3272

TABLE F-11

SORTIES (MUNITIONS) BY SEEDING SEGMENT

Munitions Types	861/862*	863	864	865	867	868	871	Misc**
WAAPM	24 (129)	9 (46)	7 (31)	11 (60)	10 (55)	6 (32)	5 (26)	8 (44)
Gravel	39 (216)	15 (82)	18 (87)	19 (135)	10 (51)	22 (106)	6 (28)	3 (12)
MK-36	8 (100)		24 (207)		24 (220)	17 (156)		
CBU-24	6 (45)	6 (24)	2 (2)	19 (151)	6 (45)	25 (204)	2 (11)	3 (19)
CBU-49	8 (52)	5 (37)	1 (4)	22 (175)	5 (37)	11 (85)	1 (4)	3 (20)
CBU-52		1 (8)	1 (8)	5 (40)	1 (7)	14 (111)	2 (4)	
MK-82	8 (84)					2 (24)	1 (7)	22 (230)
MK-84 LGB					1 (3)	2 (3)		1 (3)
M-118 LGB					1 (1)			1 (1)
Total Sorties	93	36	53	76	58	99	17	41
Total Munitions	(626)	(197)	(339)	(561)	(419)	(721)	(80)	(329)

TABLE F-12

ENEMY ACTIVITY IN ROUTE 103 AREA

Week Ending	Sensor Assessments (Veh or Pers)	Seeding Segments with Sensors	Enemy Activity Per Segment w/Sensors
24 Aug	19	5	3.80
31 Aug	13	7	1.85
7 Sep	0	7	0
14 Sep	3	7	0.43
21 Sep	33	8	4.13
28 Sep	16	8	2.00
5 Oct	28	8	3.50
12 Oct	9	8	1.10
19 Oct	3	8	0.40
26 Oct	0	8	0
2 Nov	0	8	0
10 Nov	0	8	0

TABLE F-13

ROAD CONSTRUCTION, ROUTE 103

Date of Photo Reconnaissance	Number of Kilometers of Road Completed
29 Jul	20
23 Aug	25
28 Aug	25
5 Sep	26
8 Sep	26.2
14 Sep	26.4
16 Sep	26.4
26 Sep	26.9

No more road was completed after 26 Sep 71 during Commando Hunt VI.

APPENDIX FOOTNOTES

Appendix B

1. (S) WAIS Study.
2. Ibid.
3. Ibid. Also, (TS) Commando Hunt VII Plan.
4. (S) Commando Hunt V, Appendix B. Also (S) WAIS Study.
5. (S) WAIS Study.
6. Ibid.
7. (S) WAIS Study.
8. Ibid.
9. (S) MIG Activity During Commando Hunt VI, 7AF (INODO) working paper, undated.
10. Ibid. Also, (S) WAIS Study.
11. Ibid.
12. Ibid.

Appendix C

1. (S) WAIS Study.
2. Ibid.
3. Ibid.
4. Ibid.
5. Ibid.
6. Ibid.
7. Ibid.

8.   Ibid.
9. (S) WAIS, 18 September 1971.
10. (S) WAIS, 6 November 1971.
11. (S) WAIS Study.
12.   Ibid.
13.   Ibid.
14. (TS) Commando Hunt VI Plan.
15.   Ibid.
16. (S) WAIS, 15 May and 22 May 1971.
17. (S) WAIS Study.
18. (S) WAIS, 12 June 1971.
19. (S) WAIS Study.
20.   Ibid.
21. (S) WAIS, 28 August 1971.
22.   Ibid.
23. (S) WAIS Study.
24. (S) WAIS, 25 September 1971.
25. (S) WAIS Study.
26. (S) WAIS, 23 October 1971.
27. (S) WAIS, 30 October 1971.
28. (S) WAIS, 30 October and 6 November 1971.
29. (S) WAIS Study.
30.   Ibid.
31.   Ibid.

32. Ibid.

33. (TS) Commando Hunt VI Plan.

34. Ibid.

35. (S) WAIS Study.

36. Ibid.

37. Ibid.

38. Ibid.

39. Ibid.

40. Ibid.

41. Ibid. Also, (S) Study by the author of Summary, Air Operations Southeast Asia, PACAF (DOA), May through October 1971. Also, (S) Commando Hunt V.

42. Ibid.

Appendix D

1. (S) Combat Evaluation Report, Commando Bed, 432 TRW, Udorn, December 1971.

2. Ibid.

3. Ibid.

4. (U) TAC Message, 142018Z July 1971, Subj: LUU-2/B Flare.

5. (S) Combat Evaluation Report, 7AF (DOXQM), Subj: Initial Combat Evaluation, CBU-55, 20 March 1972.

Appendix E

1. (S) Study by the author of Weather Evaluation - Southeast Asia Operations, prepared monthly by 7AF/1st Weather Wing, April - October 1971 (Weather Eval). Also, (TS) Commando Hunt VI Plan, Annex AW.

2.   <u>Ibid</u>.

3.   <u>Ibid</u>.

4. (S) Weather Eval Study.

5.   <u>Ibid</u>.

6. (S) Weather Eval, May 1971.

7.   <u>Ibid</u>, June 1971.

8.   <u>Ibid</u>, July 1971.

9.   <u>Ibid</u>, August 1971.

10.   <u>Ibid</u>, September 1971.

11.   <u>Ibid</u>, October 1971.

12. (S) Weather Eval Study.

13.   <u>Ibid</u>.

GLOSSARY

AAA	Antiaircraft artillery
AB	Air Base
ABF	Attack by fire (in RVN, referred to enemy mortar recoilless rifle, and rocket attacks against friendly installations)
AGM	Air-to-ground missile
AO	Area of Operations
Arc Light	(S) B-52 operations in SEA. Most missions flown during Commando Hunt VI were from U-Tapao, Thailand.
ARVN	Army of the Republic of Vietnam
BDA	Bomb Damage Assessment
Barrel Roll	(S) The geographic area of northern Laos
Buffalo Hunter	(S) SAC drone photographic reconnaissance operations in SEA
CINCPACAF	Commander-in-Chief, Pacific Air Forces
COMUSMACV	Commander, U.S. Military Assistance Command, Vietnam
DMZ	Demilitarized Zone
FAC	Forward Air Controller
FANK	Forces Armees Nationales Khmer (Cambodian Army) (French for Cambodian National Armed Forces)
FSB	Fire Support Base
Gravel	(C) Antipersonnel mines, depending for their effect on blast and fragmentation. Individual mines weighed less than 1/2 pound, could be detonated by an applied pressure of five pounds. ((C) 7AFRP 136-2 NO 1, Conventional Airmunitions Guide, 9 March 1972)
ICE	Initial Combat Evaluation
IGLOO WHITE	A surveillance system consisting of air-delivered sensors, relay aircraft, and an infiltration surveillance center
IDP	Interdiction Point

*In general, definitions come from (S) SEA Glossary (1961-1971), 7AF (DOAC), 31 July 1971. Notable exceptions are identified.

Intertropical Convergence Zone	The varying location where the trade winds from the Northern and Southern Hemispheres meet. It is normally north of the equator from May through October and south of the equator from November through April. (Weather Elements: A Text in Elementary Meteorology; Blair, Thomas A. & Fite, Robert C., Prentice - Hall, Inc., Englewood Cliffs, N.J. 1965)
KAF	Khmer Air Force
KBA	Killed by Air
LGB	Laser-guided bomb
LOC	Line of Communication
LS	Lima Site. Temporary aircraft landing site in Laos
MIG	Soviet jet fighter aircraft of several series designed by Mikoyan and Guevich
MR	Military Region
NVAF	North Vietnamese Air Force
NVN	North Vietnam
PACAF	Pacific Air Forces
PDJ	Plaine des Jarres. French for Plain of Jars
POL	Petroleum, Oil, and Lubricants
QRF	Quick Reaction Force
RLAF	Royal Laotian Air Force
RLG	Royal Laotian Government
RNO	Results not Observed
RVN	Republic of Vietnam
SAM	Surface-to-air Missile
SEA	Southeat Asia
SEADAB	Southeast Asia Data Base
SL	Steel Tiger
Steel Tiger	(S) The geographic area of southern Laos
Strike Aircraft	Consist of A-1, A-6, A-7, A-37, AC-47, AC-119, AC-130, B-52, B-57, F-4, F-5, F-100, F-105, and T-28
tac air	Tactical air. Includes all strike aircraft other than B-52 and special systems
TFA	Task Force Alpha. (S) A filter point for sensor information received under the IGLOO WHITE concept. Located at Nakhon Phanom RTAFB, Thailand

TIC	Troops in Contact. An engagement between Allied and enemy ground forces
USAF	United States Air Force
VNAF	South Vietnamese Air Force
VR	Visual Reconnaissance
WAAPM	(C) Wide area antipersonnel mine. Effects came from fragmentation when disturbances of automatically extended trip wires detonated the mine. A single dispenser carried 540 mines. (C) Conventional Airmunitions Guide)